TRIPLE YOUR PROFIT!

Stop Being a Profit Soldier and Start Being a Profit Winner

Practical Business Training for Hard-working Business Owners and Managers

Dr. Albert D. Bates

President, Profit Planning Group

DISCLAIMER
The purpose of this book is to educate. The author and/or publisher do not guarantee that anyone following these techniques, suggestions, tips, ideas, or strategies will engender success. The author and/or publisher shall have neither liability nor responsibility to anyone with respect to any loss or damage caused, or alleged to be caused, directly or indirectly by the information contained in this book.

Library of Congress Control Number: 2011933909

ISBN: 978-1-936449-07-1

Cover Design/Interior Layout: Ronda Taylor, www.taylorbydesign.com

Hugo House Publishers, Ltd.
Englewood, Colorado
Austin, Texas
(877) 700-0616
www.HugoHousePublishers.com

Contents

Introduction   **vii**

STEP 1

Take the Business Back from Your Accountant   **1**

Income Statement. 3

The Balance Sheet. 8

Financial Statements: How Often and How Fast 10

Moving Forward. 10

STEP 2

Set a Realistic Profit Target   **11**

Maximum Profit Level 11

Time Frame. 14

Moving Forward. 15

STEP 3

Understand Your Profit Dynamics   **17**

The Key Profit Drivers 17

Sales Increases 19

Fixed Expense Reductions 20

Gross Margin Increases. 22

Investment Reductions 23

Moving Forward. 25

STEP 4

Make Your Sales Profitably   **27**

The Payroll Challenge 27

Setting Sales and Payroll Goals 28

Growing Too Fast 33

How Do I Do That?. 35

Moving Forward. 36

STEP 5

Get Control of Your Gross Margin 37

Making It Up With Volume 37

Setting a Gross Margin Target 41

Buy Low, Sell High and Control In Between 42

Pricing For Profit 46

Putting Everything Together 48

Moving Forward 50

STEP 6

Target Your Investment Levels Properly 51

The Break-Even Point 51

The Break-Even Point and Investment Levels 55

Cash Versus Profit 57

Moving Forward 61

STEP 7

Developing a Plan 63

Reasons Not to Plan 65

The Planning Process: Thinking Backwards 67

Creating Action Programs 70

Moving Forward 70

To Do List 71

Appendix 74

Additional Resources 76

About the Author 77

Dedication

To my father and his little red wagon. An inspiration still.

Important Note: Read This Carefully

This is not just a book; it is an educational package. There are two parts to the package. You need to have (and use!) both parts to truly improve profitability:

- **The Book**—Since you are reading this, you either have it or you are clairvoyant.

- **The Excel Templates**—There are two Excel files that are essential companions to the book. They allow you to 1) tailor all of the exhibits in the book to your own firm and 2) develop a plan quickly and easily. You absolutely must have these templates loaded on your computer to get the full benefit of this package.

To obtain the templates, go to the following web site: www.profitplanninggroup.com/tripleprofit.

You will find two Excel files there. Download both to your hard drive.

- **TripleProfitExhibits**—This template has all of the exhibits and will show them with your numbers in them. You will need to print company-specific exhibits as you go through the book.

- **PlanningtoTripleProfit**—This template allows you to develop a plan. You will not need it until the end of the book.

The templates require a password to open. The password is **BigAl** and is case sensitive.

As you go through each chapter, print out the corresponding exhibits from the first template for your firm. At the end of the book use the second template to develop a financial plan that will actually increase your profit.

The Firm Versus You

This book is written in conversational language, rather than formal business language. When the discussion talks about "the firm" it is an indication that lots of companies face the profit challenges being discussed. When the discussion switches to "you" it will talk about what you and your firm need to do to improve. When it talks about you, please note the discussion carefully.

Introduction

Most business owners are victims of a work-ethic mentality. You are probably one of them. They believe that their role in life is to work long, hard hours. Interestingly, most owners actually enjoy working those long, hard hours. There is a great deal of psychic income from providing a good service or product. There is also a lot of pride in the independence that comes from being their own boss.

The problem is that too often those long, hard hours do not generate the dollar profit that should accompany the psychic income. In fact, most businesses produce inadequate profits.

Research conducted by the Profit Planning Group over the last thirty years suggests that companies of all sizes can be lumped into three profit categories:

- **Disasters**—Approximately 30% of all firms either lose money or generate profits that are so low the business really should shut down. Whenever there is a recession these are the buildings with "going out of business" signs in the window. Psychic income doesn't pay the rent.

- **Soldiers**—The vast majority of firms (around 60%) produce profits that keep them from shutting the door, but are far from adequate. To a certain extent the owners are trapped. The physic income is nice, but the profits are not. After working for 40 years, what is the result?

- **Winners**—The top 10% of firms generate sensational profits. On top of that, they also get that wonderful psychic income.

It's actually worse then just inadequate profits today. Firms that don't produce strong profits can't be sold in the future for anything other than fire-sale prices. At retirement time there is no residual value to the business.

There is some good news, though. The Winners are not any smarter or any harder working than the other 90% of the firms. They have simply put in place the programs and practices that ensure profits today and into the future. They are doing nothing that cannot be done by everybody else.

The difference in profits between the Winners and the other firms is not small. The Winners inevitably produce two, three or even four times the profit of the Soldiers, even on the same sales volume.

This book has one goal. That is to take the stack of dollars that *you* produce for yourself each year and make it three times as high. In doing so you will continue to produce the same psychic income and the same level of independence. You are simply adding to that psychic income the financial reward you deserve.

As was stated above, producing higher profits is challenging, but not overwhelming. At the same time, it is far from automatic. If it were automatic, then the Winners would be more than 10% of all firms.

If you are going to become a profit Winner, you have to be willing to rethink *everything* your firm does. Be aware that everything means everything. You must be willing to abandon everything you have been told about how to increase your profit in the past. You must also be willing to read this book in detail and use the Excel template that comes with it.

There are seven steps that have to be taken to get to high-profit levels. This book is organized into those steps rather than being organized into chapters. For the remainder of this book, everything will be personalized at some point. This is what *you* have to do to make more money to build a better life for your family:

- **Step One**—Take the business back from your accountant
- **Step Two**—Set a realistic profit target
- **Step Three**—Understand your profit dynamics
- **Step Four**—Make your sales profitably
- **Step Five**—Get control of your gross margin
- **Step Six**—Target your investment levels properly
- **Step Seven**—Run your business with a plan

If you don't want to bother spending some significant time with this book to fully understand what you have to do to create three times the profits, a suggestion is in order: Get a comfortable job at the Department of Motor Vehicles. Otherwise, time to stop talking and start doing.

Load the Excel template on to the hard drive of your computer and turn the page.

Take the Business Back from Your Accountant

Most of the people who start and run small to medium-sized businesses are not accountants. They are people who have the guts to take a risk. They are also the folks who only remember that debits were against the windows and credits were against the wall in Accounting 101.

In short, finance is a foreign language for the overwhelming majority of small business owners. Most likely this includes you. Consequently, your accountant handles all of the financial stuff and occasionally tells you how you are doing.

Note this carefully: Your accountant doesn't know jack about how to increase the profits of your business. In fact, the original working title of this book was *Fire Your Accountant!* Since your accountant probably has a family, you should not resort to firing. You should simply put your accountant on a very short leash. Remember that you are the owner and the decision maker, so your accountant must do what you want when you want it.

In the end, your accountant will prove very useful after you have read this book and successfully implemented the concepts. Namely, your accountant will work to keep you from paying too much in taxes on all that profit.

Stop Everything

Two Excel templates came with this book. By now you should have loaded the first template onto your hard drive and entered some basic information for your firm. This simple exercise allows you to have every exhibit in this book tailored to your company.

Load the blasted Excel template, now.

Throughout this book there will be exhibits for a typical small business. Calling that firm Typical Company or Sample Company seems a little impersonal. Consequently, the company will be Mountain View. (The author lives in Colorado and thinks the name is clever.)

Mountain View is both completely different from your business and exactly like your business. That is why the Excel template is so powerful. It allows you to look at every exhibit for your company's specific situation.

Be assured that every concept, idea and conclusion regarding Mountain View also applies to your business. The numbers will be different, but not the concepts. Making money is making money.

Income Statement

The primary financial statement that you need from your accountant is an income statement. You probably get one every month or so. Maybe only once a quarter or even once a year. Whatever the frequency, there is just one small problem. What you get sucks swamp water big time.

Exhibit 1 provides the structure you should demand from your accountant. It has two major differences from what you now get. Before looking at the differences, let's make sure you are fully aware of all of the terms and what they mean.

- **Net Sales**—The revenue the firm generates. In the example, Mountain View has brought in $5.0 million. It includes the sale of all products and services, less any discounts or allowances given to customers.

- **Cost of Goods Sold**—How much the firm paid for the stuff that it sold. Do not let your accountant tell you it is anything else. If you sold something, you had to buy it from somebody. Cost of goods can include both the cost of merchandise and the cost of labor if your firm sells services. For Mountain View, every $1.00 in sales costs the firm $.75.

- **Gross Margin**—Simply the difference between what you sell things for and what you buy them for. In this case, every $1.00 of sales revenue produced $.25 to cover expenses and generate a profit.

- **Expenses**—What it costs you to run the business. In Exhibit 1 expenses are broken into payroll and everything else. Payroll is always the name of the game from an expense perspective. In fact, payroll is a lot larger than all of the other expenses combined. Total expenses eat up 23.0% of all sales revenue generated.

- **Profit Before Taxes**—This is what you get to keep after paying all of the expenses. In order to compare different firms, profit before taxes is used. Like many businesses, Mountain View produces a puny 2.0% bottom line. Every $1.00 in sales results in only 2¢ in profit. Too much work for not enough profit.

Exhibit 1
Mountain View, Inc.
Income Statement

	Dollars	Percent of Sales
Net Sales	$5,000,000	100.0
Cost of Goods Sold	3,750,000	75.0
Gross Margin	1,250,000	25.0
Expenses		
Owner's Compensation	60,000	1.2
All Other Payroll and Fringe Benefits	690,000	13.8
Total Payroll and Fringe Benefits	750,000	15.0
All Other Expenses	400,000	8.0
Total Expenses	1,150,000	23.0
Profit Before Taxes	$100,000	2.0

Alternative Expense Analysis

	Dollars	Percent of Sales
Fixed Expenses	$900,000	18.0
Variable Expenses	$250,000	5.0

What You Need to Know About the Numbers:

- Owner's Compensation is *not* your actual salary and fringe benefits. It is what an outsider would be paid to manage the business.

- All Other Payroll and Fringe Benefits covers all other payroll costs in the firm, including salaries, commissions, overtime and the like.

- All Other Expenses is everything that is not payroll or fringe benefits.

- Fixed Expenses only change when the firm takes some specific action, such as hiring an employee.

- Variable Expenses change automatically as sales change.

The only advantage of having such a small bottom line is that the taxes are low. There isn't much to tax. Not a great claim to fame. It needs to get better.

Okay, so how is this income statement different from what you get? As stated earlier, there are two differences: 1) your compensation, and 2) the addition of an analysis of fixed and variable expenses.

1) Your Compensation. The payroll category must include a line item for the salary, health insurance and retirement benefits that the firm would have to pay an outsider to come in and run the business if the owner weren't there. No more, no less.

Note that if you are a manager rather than an owner, then your compensation is already at the market level. There is no need to make an adjustment.

This is absolutely not the salary, health insurance and retirement benefits the owner actually receives. The actual number is immaterial for calculating profit. This seems a little strange. It is not; it is one of the keys to driving higher profit.

Most small businesses are S Corporations, partnerships, LLCs or proprietorships. This means that there is almost never a realistic line for the owner's salary and fringe benefits. The salary and fringe benefits are mixed up with profit. That must stop.

Sometimes there is no salary line for the owner at all. Everything is in profit. In other instances the payroll line for the owner represents a draw against profit. It is based upon how much the owner needs to cover the mortgage and other personal expenses. Neither approach is helpful in planning profit. Actually, both approaches are harmful.

The reason this is critical is that you have to determine a true salary and fringe benefits number in order to figure out what your profit really is. This might get a little bit more into accounting stuff than you would like. However, it is also life and death, so…

Suppose the owner of Mountain View has talked to bankers, friends, trade associations, etc. and has determined that total compensation for the owner/executive of a business of this size should be $60,000. Again, this includes salary, health insurance and the retirement package. This is the compensation figure used in Exhibit 1. It is a completely clean and accurate income statement. The owner knows exactly how the firm is performing.

However, suppose the firm is an S Corporation and therefore does not show owner's compensation on the income statement. The $60,000 would replaced with $0. Assuming that the other expenses are the same, the income statement would report a profit of $160,000. That is a dramatic overstatement. The only reason the profit is so high is because the owner worked for free.

Time for a slightly different scenario. Assume that all of the other expenses in aggregate are $60,000 higher so that profit is the same $100,000 shown in Exhibit 1. However, the owner's salary is still at $0.

In this instance the income statement is really lying to the owner. The *actual* profit is only $40,000 (the $100,000 reported minus $60,000 that should have been shown as compensation). It is absolutely essential to show a market rate of compensation so that the true profit can be measured.

Wait, it gets worse. In many small businesses the husband runs the business and the wife takes care of inventory and pays the employees. (This is not meant to be sexist, it is a reality.) The wife also teaches school during the day and does her clerical work for the company at night for free. Wow!

Guess what? The firm is violating the 13th Amendment to the United States Constitution. That's the one that outlaws slavery and involuntary servitude. Everybody must get paid. The income statement must reflect the value of all of the labor provided by a spouse or kids. If the firm can't afford to pay them, it isn't a business.

Starting today: Show owner's compensation as a separate line on the income statement accurately reflecting local market wages and benefits. Your accountant will balk and point out, correctly, that this doesn't follow traditional accounting rules.

If your account balks too much, fire your accountant. Yes, he is your brother-in-law. Fire him anyway. He works for you.

A Technical Note on Two Sets of Books

Everything discussed here is designed to help you produce a profit-based income statement. This is perfectly legal. This is the statement that will tell you how you are really doing. Your accountant will keep another set of books that reflects IRS filing requirements and the like. That is not only fine, it is required by law. That set of books will show whatever salary you desire and as much in retirement benefits as the law will allow. However, if you don't know how the business is doing, you can't make it better. The profit-based income statement is the one you must use to manage your business.

---

2) Fixed and Variable Expenses. This is simply a different way of looking at the expenses. The expenses do not change in total. In Exhibit 1 total expenses are still $1,150,000. In this analysis, they are merely split into different categories that are more useful for planning.

Fixed Expenses can be thought of as overhead expenses. The real key is that they do not change during this fiscal year unless the firm takes some action or agrees to some action taken by others. If the firm hires a new permanent employee it has increased its fixed expenses. If the landlord raises the rent, and the firm agrees to it, then again the fixed expenses have increased.

Next year, fixed expenses will probably be higher. Employees will want raises, landlords will probably raise the rent, utility bills will increase and the like. However, until the end of this year these expenses will remain the same each month.

The implication of fixed expenses is that the firm knows how much they are going to be ahead of time. Now, the lease may call for an increase in rent in the middle of the year. Assuming the lease has been read, management knows about the increase before the year starts. The rent is one level for six months and another level for the second six month period. The key is that fixed expenses are known in advance. They are constant regardless of the level of sales.

Variable Expenses are the ones that go up or down *automatically* as sales change. For example, many firms have a sales force that is paid a commission based upon sales. If sales go up, there are more commissions.

Similarly, if the firm allows customers to pay by credit card, the firm has to pay a percentage of the transaction to the credit card processing company. More credit card sales, more fees.

> ### A Sneak Preview
> Every firm has two problems that will be shown on the income statement:
> - The gross margin is too low
> - The payroll expense is too high
>
> They may also have a sales problem, but they definitely have the two above. This will be covered in detail in Step Three. Be ready.

The Balance Sheet

Unfortunately, the balance sheet is the dullest financial statement in the history of the free world. However, it is important, so forgive a few paragraphs.

Exhibit 2 presents the balance sheet for Mountain View. It provides three important bits of information: 1) how much money is invested in the business, 2) what it is invested in, and 3) how much money the owners have personally invested in the business.

1) How Much Is Invested. The Total Assets line is the one that indicates (translated from accounting) the total amount of money invested in the business. In the case of Mountain View there is $1,000,000 invested.

2) What It Is Invested In. It looks like accounts receivable and inventory are the two big items in terms of investment. Accounts receivable shows how much customers owe for the things they bought but haven't yet paid for. Inventory is the cost value of all the merchandise in stock.

3) How Much The Owners Have Invested. The line called Net Worth (or equity) is the investment in the business made by the owners. It consists of all the money initially invested plus all of the profit that has been made (if any) that was not taken out of the business.

These are the key components of the balance sheet. That's enough for now. There are a few other things that would also be nice to know, but they can wait.

Exhibit 2
Mountain View, Inc.
Balance Sheet

Assets	Dollars	Percent of Total
Cash	$50,000	5.0
Accounts Receivable	300,000	30.0
Inventory	400,000	40.0
Other Current Assets	50,000	5.0
Total Current Assets	800,000	80.0
Fixed Assets	200,000	20.0
Total Assets	$1,000,000	100.0
Liabilities and Net Worth		
Accounts Payable	$250,000	25.0
Other Current Liabilities	100,000	10.0
Total Current Liabilities	350,000	35.0
Long-Term Liabilities	50,000	5.0
Total Liabilities	400,000	40.0
Net Worth	600,000	60.0
Total Liabilities and Net Worth	$1,000,000	100.0

What You Need to Know About the Numbers:

- Total Assets is the total amount of money invested in the business.

- Net Worth is how much money **you** have invested in the business.

Financial Statements: How Often and How Fast

Time to drive your accountant nuts. You need to receive financial statements (a profit-based income statement and a balance sheet) every month and you need them no later than three days after the month ends. If you are going to stay on top of the business, you must work in real time.

Your accountant will tell you it can't be done. Tell the accountant to do it. End of story. With current technology there is no excuse.

Moving Forward

You need an income statement, balance sheet and a few key ratios on the third day following every month-end. These statements need to show your compensation based upon local labor-market conditions. This is not your actual compensation. It is the market value of your time. With this approach you can actually tell if you earned an adequate profit or not.

Once you have this information, you can go on to the next big step. Namely, determining how much profit the income statement should show every month.

STEP

2

Set a Realistic Profit Target

Whenever the owners of small to medium-sized businesses are asked how much profit their firm should generate, they always come up with the same two answers:

"As much as we can."

"More than we do now."

Neither of these is particularly helpful. If the firm is going to reach its full profit potential, it has to know what that potential is. Neither "more" nor "lots" provides the specificity that is required.

There are two components to setting a profit goal. Both need to be given very careful attention:

- **Maximum Profit Level**—This is determining the highest realistic profit level that can be produced. This is measured in terms of profit before taxes as a percent of net sales. In Exhibit 1 it was noted that Mountain View currently has a profit margin of 2.0% of sales. The Maximum Profit Level is what the firm could produce if everything were properly planned and controlled. It might be 5.0% or 10.0% or any other number.

- **Time Frame**—This involves determining how fast the firm should be able to reach the Maximum Profit Level. For some firms it might be one or two years; for others it might be closer to five years.

Maximum Profit Level

Determining the Maximum Profit Level involves a very precise process which is outlined in **Exhibit 3**. At the conclusion of that precise process a degree of judgment is required. Do not be bothered by the fact that the process is part science and part judgment. The science portion will rule.

In determining the Maximum Profit Level the profit figure must always be after paying fair compensation to the owner. In short, the firm needs to produce that fair compensation *plus* the Maximum Profit Level number.

Exhibit 3 rests upon two guidelines that can be supported by empirical observation. That means there is a lot of very good, hard evidence to support the guidelines provided in Exhibit 3. That evidence was gathered across a broad spectrum of industries over many years. The exhibit is not arbitrary.

Exhibit 3
Mountain View, Inc.
Setting a Goal for the Maximum Profit Level

Profit Goal #1

1. Total Assets	Actual Number	$1,000,000
2. Return on Assets Goal	Realistic Return	20.0%
3. Profit Goal #1 (Before Taxes)	[1 x 2]	$200,000

Profit Goal #2

4. Gross Margin	Actual Number	$1,250,000
5. Return on Gross Margin Goal	Realistic Return	25.0%
6. Profit Goal #2 (Before Taxes)	[4 x 5]	$312,500

Profit Goal #3

7. The Two Goals Added Together	[3 + 6]	$512,500
8. Average (Profit Goals #1 and #2 divided by 2)		$256,250

The Three Goals for the Maximum Profit Level
As a Percent of Sales

9. Net Sales	Actual Number	$5,000,000
10. ROA Method (#1)	[3 ÷ 9]	4.0%
11. ROGM Method (#2)	[6 ÷ 9]	6.3%
12. Average (#3)	[8 ÷ 9]	5.1%

The Maximum Profit Level represents the sort of results produced by the winners—the top 10% of the firms in terms of profit performance. There is no need to bother with what the other 90% of the firms do.

The first guideline is that in most industries the high-profit firms produce a Return on Assets of around 20.0%. In some industries the Return on Assets is a little higher, in some it is a little lower. It is, though, a strong general guideline.

The second guideline is that the high-profit firms tend to produce a profit that is around 25.0% of the gross margin generated by the firm. Again, in some industries profit is higher; in others it is lower. This is a second guideline.

Stop Everything Again

The Excel template that came with this book will perform the calculations for you in Exhibit 3 in less than a second. The purpose of Exhibit 3 here is so that you have an awareness of the process. Never trust the computer until you know what it is doing. When you finish Exhibit 3 you will be driving the Excel template, not riding shotgun.

Exhibit 3 uses the numbers for Mountain View. In the first three steps a dollar profit goal is set based upon the 20.0% Return on Assets target mentioned before. The next three steps also set a dollar profit goal using the Return on Gross Margin target. After that, the two different goals are averaged to produce yet a third goal.

At the bottom the three dollar goals are converted to a percent of sales. This is absolutely essential. During the course of the year you will be reviewing an income statement that presents profit as a percent of sales. You need to track your actual results against a goal based upon this ratio.

As a reminder, the three goals are for the Maximum Profit Level the firm can be expected to achieve over time. The profit goals are always in addition to the compensation that the owner receives. That compensation, in turn, is equal to what an outsider would have to be paid.

If you completed Exhibit 3 for your firm, you now have three goals. Good luck. No, seriously—good luck. The two procedures will give you two somewhat different answers. If you are in a high-investment industry, Return on Assets is preferred. Otherwise, feel free to select the average or the highest. Don't even think about selecting the lowest.

Time Frame

You need to remember a couple of your mother's favorite homilies.
"Rome wasn't built in a day."
"Slow but steady wins the race."
These are essential thoughts for deciding how fast you can get to where you want to be. It always takes longer than you think it should.

In determining how fast you can reach the Maximum Profit Level you need to resolve two conflicting issues. First, your firm has to stretch or it will never get to where it wants to be. Second, if your goals are too high you create a climate in which goals are never met so they don't really matter. Both conditions are fatal.

1) Stretch Performance. Almost every firm can do better than it is currently doing. In order to eventually reach the Maximum Profit Level you need to push the envelope a little on profit performance every single year. Your goals need to be challenging.

2) Reaching the Goal. Too high of a goal is just as bad as too low. If you set an overly aggressive goal, then the firm will not reach it. That sends a message to everybody in the company that goals are just arbitrary numbers. Next year you will set a new goal and you won't reach that either.

You have to create an atmosphere in which tough goals are set and tough goals are met. For most firms your pre-tax profit margin can be improved by somewhere between .5% and 1.5% in a single year depending upon whether the economy is good or bad, you catch some good luck or bad, and the like. Over time, it works out to about 1.0% per year.

If you recall, Mountain View currently has a profit margin of 2.0%. Ultimately, according to Exhibit 3, it would like to get to somewhere between 5.0% and 6.0%. Using the 6.0% goal, getting there will probably take somewhere very close to four years. Profit should be 3.0% the coming year, 4.0% the year after and so on.

If the economy is sluggish at the start, the firm might choose 2.5% next year. Management could then reevaluate the situation in subsequent years. The essential ingredient is that every year sees some improvement.

Help! We are losing money right now. For firms that are losing money, the answer is simple. Get to break even in one year and then start ratcheting up slowly.

If you can't get to break even in a single year, give some serious consideration to liquidating your business. You are destroying the capital that you have invested. Go find a job working for somebody else.

Moving Forward

You should now know your Maximum Profit Level. You should also have an idea about how fast you can get there. There is still one little bitty minor matter left. How are you going to do that? Stay tuned.

Understand Your Profit Dynamics

There is an old management saying, "The way to make more money is to do more of the things that are good for you and less of the things that are bad for you." Like all old management sayings, it is brilliant in concept, but says nothing about how to do it.

The problem with running a business is that everything is important. Driving more sales would certainly be good for you. So would lowering expenses. Collecting receivables faster looks nice, too. There are more good things than can be done in a day.

In addition, there are a lot of things that have to be done whether they are good for you are not. Payroll checks really need to be written on time, reports have to be sent to the IRS and so on. The list is endless.

In small to medium-sized businesses a very few people, or even one person, has to do all of this. As a result, priorities are difficult to set. Even when priorities are set, they are not necessarily based upon what really drives more profit. In many cases the priorities become those tasks the owner enjoys doing most.

If you are ever going to reach the Maximum Profit Level, you need a brand new set of priorities. They must be set based upon the things that drive profit to the bottom line the quickest. With the right priorities, it still may be a four to five year journey to where you want to be. With the wrong priorities it is a never-ending journey.

The Key Profit Drivers

The process of setting profit priorities can be helped along by looking at the four graphs in Exhibits 4 through 7. The exhibits look at what are often called the Key Profit Drivers. These are the factors that are most important in improving your financial results.

The exhibits show how fast changes in each Key Profit Driver will cause bottom-line performance (PBT%) to improve. Even though there are four graphs, they look at five drivers. The last graph does double duty and gives you two for the price of one:

- **Sales**—Increasing sales volume without increasing the fixed expenses. Remember that variable expenses go up automatically, so sales only need to be leveraged against the fixed expenses.
- **Fixed Expenses**—Reducing the level of fixed expenses in the business without reducing the level of sales volume. Cost cutting without sales cutting.
- **Gross Margin**—Increasing the gross margin dollars in the firm without increasing the sales volume. This would come from those two legendary favorites, buying low and selling high.
- **Inventory**—Reducing the level of inventory investment without lowering sales.
- **Accounts Receivable**—Lowering the level of accounts receivable without a negative impact on sales.

Since some firms have no inventory and some firms have no accounts receivable, these two have been combined into one exhibit. They also turn out to be the least important items, so they can jolly well share a graph.

The exhibits present information for America's favorite company, Mountain View. Without knowing anything at all about your company, it can be stated with 100% certainty that your graphs will look very similar. There are some universal concepts in driving higher profits.

Before trying to draw some conclusions from the graphs, it is essential that you understand their structure. All four of the graphs are identical in the way information is presented.

For every graph the vertical axis represents profit before taxes as a percent of net sales (PBT%). If you recall, Mountain View wanted to get to a 6.0% bottom line. Consequently, every graph is scaled up to 6.0%. The graph starts with Mountain View's current PBT% of 2.0%.

The horizontal axis shows improvements ranging from 5.0% to 25.0%. That means that on the gross margin graph, for example, the gross margin dollars are increased by 5.0% all the way to 25.0%. Similarly on the inventory graph, the dollar amount of inventory on hand is reduced from 5.0% to 25.0%.

While the graphs are structured the same, the slopes of the lines are very different. It is essential to understand this in order to get your profit priorities in order.

Sales Increases

Yet another homily: "Sales solves all problems." In reality, increasing sales volume does solve a lot of problems. But, at the same time it actually creates some other problems. The issue of problems solved and problems created will be deferred until Step Four. The real concern at this time is how quickly more sales puts more money on the bottom line.

Exhibit 4 graphs the relationship between a sales increase and the PBT%. To reiterate, as sales increase, the fixed expenses remain constant, but the variable expenses increase at the same rate as sales volume. That is, they remain at 5.0% of sales.

This line is relatively steep. That means that as sales increase, profit dollars flow to the bottom line at a relatively fast rate. The most important thing to note about Exhibit 4 is that in order to get to the 6.0% Maximum Profit Level by sales increases alone, sales will have to increase by more than the 25.0% end point of the graph. It looks to be something around 30.0%.

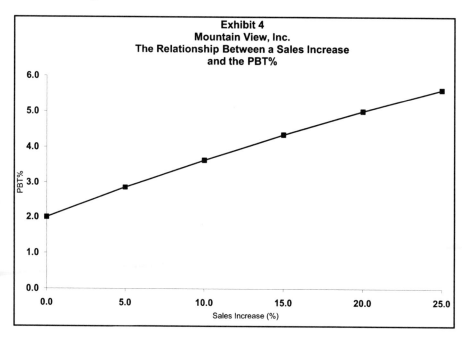

Exhibit 4
Mountain View, Inc.
The Relationship Between a Sales Increase and the PBT%

Two problems. First, 30.0% is pretty large, so increasing sales alone may not be the answer. Second, the 30.0% increase in sales must be produced without increasing the fixed expenses at all. That is almost certainly an unrealistic objective.

If you can increase your sales by 30.0% without increasing your fixed expenses, I have a suggestion for you: Fire 30.0% of your employees. Nobody has that much excess capacity lying around in their businesses.

At slower growth rates, say 5.0%, then it probably is possible to increase sales without an increase in the expense structure. Determining how much sales can increase before the expense structure becomes unhinged will be discussed in detail in Step Four of the planning process.

In short, sales growth remains an important driver of profitability. However, its impact is much less dramatic than generally thought, and it is less important than a couple of other Key Profit Drivers.

What If I Don't Believe Any of This?

Cynical aren't you. Actually, almost everything demonstrated in Step Three is counter intuitive in nature. You should demand proof. Proof is presented in the Appendix. At some point you should review it. For now, assume the graphs are correct. Keep reading through Step Three in its entirety in one reading if at all possible.

Fixed Expense Reductions

Exhibit 5 looks at the other side of the coin. Specifically, it examines the strategy of reducing fixed expenses. As always there is an important assumption: namely, the reduction in fixed expenses will not cause sales to fall.

The situation is very similar to the problem shown earlier with increasing sales. When small reductions are made, it is probably a pretty good assumption that sales will not fall. However, when the reductions in fixed expenses get large, all bets are off.

Fixed expense reductions have to be addressed from two perspectives. The first is the impact that such a reduction will have on the bottom line. (Shown in Exhibit 5. The second is the psychological impact on the firm. That is more of a touchy, feely sort of issue.

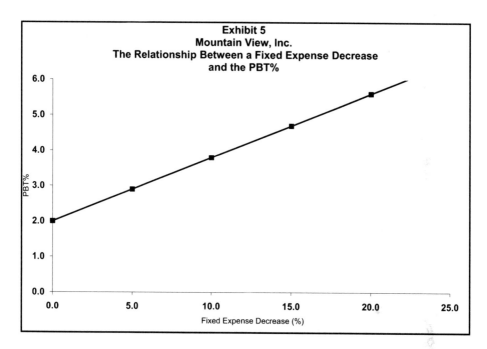

Exhibit 5
Mountain View, Inc.
The Relationship Between a Fixed Expense Decrease
and the PBT%

1) Bottom Line Impact. While looking at Exhibit 5, it is necessary to recall something from Exhibit 4. In that exhibit the line reached the target 6.0% PBT when sales increased by somewhere around 30.0%. In Exhibit 5, that goal is reached when fixed expenses are reduced by around 22.5%.

All that means is that fixed expense reductions have a larger impact on the PBT% than do sales increases. In slightly different terms, the line in Exhibit 5 goes up faster than the line in Exhibit 4.

The first response of almost everybody is that this can't be right. Surely sales must be the key driver of profitability. The answer is no. Sales is important. However, in terms of how quickly the PBT% can be increased, fixed expense reductions are even more significant.

2) Psychological Impact. Expense reductions are the victims of very bad PR. The general perception is that reducing expenses is a sign of failure. While increasing sales implies that the firm is going forward, decreasing expenses is almost always viewed as going backwards.

This psychological barrier must be overcome. Expense reductions, if implemented properly, are fundamental to reaching the mystical Maximum Profit Level. You can't get there without some expense control.

In Step Four, the concept of sales increases and expense reductions will be brought together. To use a hackneyed consulting term, they are two halves of the same canoe. They need to be planned together. For now, though, it is essential to keep in mind that controlling expenses is just a little bit more powerful than increasing sales in terms of improving the PBT%.

Gross Margin Increases

Now for one of the most important revelations in profit planning. Gross margin is the single most important driver of profitability. Nothing else comes close.

Exhibit 6 demonstrates this by presenting the relationship between increasing gross margin dollars, without an increase in sales, and the PBT%. As can be seen, this is the steepest line seen to date. It is the steepest line that you will ever see in this book.

Time to review and put things into context. It took a 30.0% sales increase for Mountain View to get to a 6.0% bottom line. It only took a 22.5% fixed expense reduction to get to the same 6.0% level. For gross

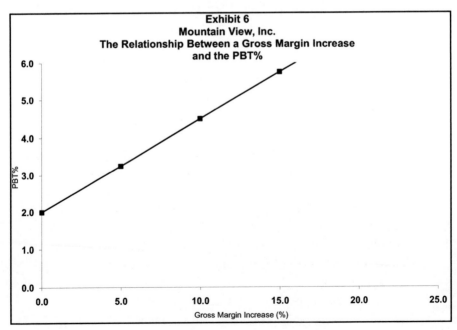

margin, the magical 6.0% level is achieved with only a 17.0% increase in gross margin dollars.

At the risk of being redundant, the exhibit incorporates the same sort of assumptions as the previous exhibits. For Exhibit 4 sales were increased without an increase in fixed expenses. For Exhibit 5, fixed expenses were decreased without reducing sales.

For Exhibit 6 the assumption is that gross margin dollars are increased on the same level of sales volume. Gross margin dollars increase but sales do not. This means that the gross margin percentage on each dollar of sales is higher.

Gross margin improvement is wonderful in terms of how fast it produces additional profit. At the same time, gross margin is probably the most challenging of all the profit drivers to get right. It's the biggest bang for the buck, but the most difficult to implement.

This is the way the world works for almost everything. If it were easy, everybody would do it. Given the importance of gross margin, it will have an entire step in the profitability process devoted to it.

Investment Reductions

Easily the most misunderstood driver of profitability is investment control. It turns out that reducing inventory and accounts receivable (assuming the firm has these investments) produces almost no improvement in the bottom line.

Exhibit 7 employs the same approach as before. The investment in either inventory or accounts receivable is reduced by up to 25.0%. The impact on the PBT% is then shown on the horizontal axis. Realistically, the lines could be called flat. That is, decreasing the level of investment in either category produces almost no gain in profitability.

When investment factors are reduced, there are two major cost savings. The first, and most obvious, is interest expense. With less investment there is less need to borrow money. If the firm doesn't borrow to begin with, then less investment creates an opportunity to invest funds in certificates of deposit or something else.

The second cost savings is that having less investment reduces some other costs as well. In the case of accounts receivable, with a lowered investment there is likely to be a reduction in bad debts. There should also be a reduction in the costs associated with hounding customers.

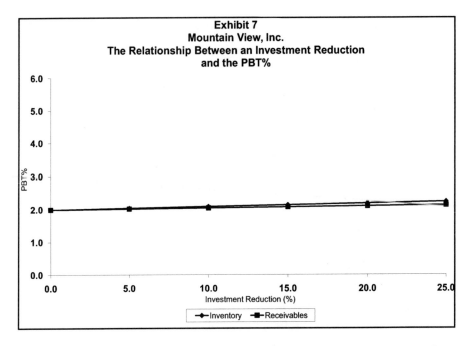

Exhibit 7
Mountain View, Inc.
The Relationship Between an Investment Reduction
and the PBT%

Inventory investment reductions demonstrate the same general situation. With less inventory there tends to be a modest reduction in obsolescence and a few other costs. The complete details of these costs have been relegated to the Appendix.

Investment control exhibits a theme that has surfaced before. Lowering inventory and accounts receivable could lower sales. This was also true of fixed expenses as an example. However, with inventory and accounts receivable the chance of a sales reduction is much greater.

If the firm sells things (as opposed to people's time) then customers expect those things to be available when they want to buy them. If the firm has absolutely nothing on hand then there are absolutely no sales. As a logical extension, fewer things on hand probably translates fewer sales. By the same token if credit terms are overly tight, credit customers may not be able to buy.

There is also one other major difference regarding inventory and accounts receivable. Too much investment creates some serious cash-flow issues. Setting investment levels to their optimal level is a challenging undertaking. The process will be discussed in much greater detail in Step Six.

Moving Forward

It is absolutely essential that you understand the size and nature of the key profit drivers in your business. The size issue is easy:

- **Gross Margin**—The big enchilada of profit determination
- **Fixed Expenses**—Also a very strong driver of profitability
- **Sales**—Relatively important as a profit driver, but slightly less important than fixed expenses and much less important than gross margin
- **Investment Levels**—Modest impact on profitability

Now that the profit relationships are understood, it is time to look at how these factors should be controlled. That will take you through the next three steps of the profit planning process.

Make Your Sales Profitably

Way back in Step One, there was something called a sneak preview. It suggested that almost every business has two problems:

- The gross margin is too low
- The payroll expense is too high

In Step Three two more suggestions were made:

- Sales increases have a relatively large impact on the bottom line
- Expense reductions have an even larger impact

It is time to put these somewhat disjointed thoughts together into a single action program. The net result will be a very specific suggestion as to how the sales and expense portions of your business should be tied together.

The Payroll Challenge

Two different expense breakouts have been discussed previously. The first was fixed versus variable. This is extremely useful in understanding volume sensitivity, how increases in sales produce higher profits. The second was payroll versus all other expenses.

In planning sales and expenses it is essential to utilize the payroll versus all other expenses breakout. There is a very important reason for this which you have to understand and appreciate.

The Profit Planning Group has conducted financial benchmarking surveys for more than thirty years. That means it has gathered a data bank of profit and loss data for more than 10,000 firms going back almost to the dark ages.

Over the course of those thirty years, payroll as a percent of sales has remained virtually constant across every industry and for almost every firm. The ratio has gone up and down slightly depending upon economic conditions. However, if the variability due to economic conditions is removed, the results are the same today as they were long ago.

On the face of it, this seems impossible. The improvements in technology during the last thirty years are nothing short of amazing. Firms are much more sophisticated today than they were way back then.

Big Deal! The data clearly show that technology has not resulted in any appreciable improvement in payroll control. Over the long term, sales and payroll tend to be tied at the hip. It is a situation that you have no choice but to change if you want to reach your Maximum Profit Level.

A moment of philosophical reflection: Doing something that has seldom been done in the last thirty years is probably going to prove extremely difficult. It certainly is if the firm decides that advances in technology and new productivity tools are the only answers to the payroll problem. Well, they aren't. An entirely different approach is required.

Setting Sales and Payroll Goals

The only way to make sales and expense control work for you is to plan and control them in conjunction with each other. The reasons for this are clear. Sales volume by itself doesn't mean doodly-squat. Payroll expense by itself doesn't mean diddly.

Highly technical terms like doodly-squat and diddly need an explanation. That explanation is facilitated by **Exhibit 8** which looks at sales and payroll together. To the surprise of absolutely nobody in the world at this point, the exhibit focuses on Mountain View.

The first column of numbers is simply the current results for Mountain View as we have come to know it and to love it. Sales are an impressive $5,000,000, but profit is a somewhat less than stellar $100,000. That means a PBT% of only 2.0% of revenue.

The next three columns examine the specific improvement that needs to be made with regard to sales and expenses. They do so under some very different assumptions about sales growth. Despite the sales growth differences, the same underlying process is taking place in each column.

The very first assumption about sales growth is that sales increase by 5.0%, from $5,000,000 now to $5,250,000 next year. It is an arbitrary

Dollar Performance	Current Results	5% Sales Growth	10% Sales Growth	5% Sales Decline
	Exhibit 8			
	Mountain View, Inc.			
	The Impact of Different Levels of Sales Growth			
	When Payroll is Properly Controlled			
Net Sales	$5,000,000	$5,250,000	$5,500,000	$4,750,000
Cost of Goods Sold	3,750,000	3,937,500	4,125,000	3,562,500
Gross Margin	1,250,000	1,312,500	1,375,000	1,187,500
Expenses				
Payroll and Fringe Benefits	750,000	772,500	810,000	697,500
All Other Expenses	400,000	420,000	440,000	380,000
Total Expenses	1,150,000	1,192,500	1,250,000	1,077,500
Profit Before Taxes	$100,000	$120,000	$125,000	$110,000
Percent of Sales Performance				
Net Sales	100.0	100.0	100.0	100.0
Cost of Goods Sold	75.0	75.0	75.0	75.0
Gross Margin	25.0	25.0	25.0	25.0
Expenses				
Payroll and Fringe Benefits	15.0	14.7	14.7	14.7
All Other Expenses	8.0	8.0	8.0	8.0
Total Expenses	23.0	22.7	22.7	22.7
Profit Before Taxes	2.0	2.3	2.3	2.3

growth rate. Just go with it for right now. Other growth rates will be explored in the other columns.

What is not specifically stated, but can be calculated from the information provided, is that while sales are increasing by 5.0%, payroll is only increasing by 3.0%. That means payroll grows from $750,000 to $772,500. This is exactly 3.0%.

Now to get really complicated. The difference between sales growth and payroll growth is 2.0 percentage points (5.0% sales growth and 3.0% payroll growth. To keep the text simple this 2.0 percentage point difference simply will be referred to as a 2.0% wedge.

This number absolutely did not just pop up randomly. In fact, this is the first item on the "To Do" list for your firm. You need to have a sales to payroll wedge of 2.0%. Feel free to write it down, paint it on the wall of your office, or tattoo it on your left forearm. What the heck, post it on Facebook. It is that important. It absolutely needs to be an unassailable goal.

How long do you have to do this? Easy answer. Every year until your firm reaches its Maximum Profit Level. At that point you can kick back.

"To Do" Number One

Generate a 2.0% sales to payroll wedge regardless of how much your sales increase or decrease.

It was suggested earlier that sales volume by itself does not mean doodly-squat. The third column of numbers attempts to demonstrate why that is so.

This column assumes that sales grow by 10.0%. Now you're talking. This is what "Masters of the Universe" do—increase that top-line number. You get to go to the club and brag about how fast your company is growing. Buy a round of drinks for everyone while you are there.

This column also assumes that a 10.0% sales increase is going to require another employee to help with the additional activity associated with higher sales. As a result, payroll expense increases by 8.0% in this column. To make sure the math is clear, payroll increases from the original $750,000 to $810,000, which is, indeed, 8.0%. The wedge between sales growth and payroll growth is once again 2.0%.

Profit does go up between the 5.0% sales growth column and the 10.0% sales growth one. To be precise, it increased from $120,000 to $125,000. While an increase is an increase, the firm had to drive another $250,000 in sales to generate the very small additional profit. The vast majority of the profit increase arose from the original 2.0% wedge between sales growth and payroll growth.

At this point as an astute reader you probably have a brilliant idea. Why not have sales go up 10.0% as shown in the third column of numbers and payroll only go up 3.0% as in the second column? A 7.0% wedge. Bingo Bob! Profit rolls in.

It's a great idea. There is one small problem. It can't be done. Other than that it is absolutely sensational. Why can't it be done? Remember that financial benchmarking studies indicate that most firms have made no improvements in payroll control in the last thirty years. A 2.0% wedge is hard enough to produce; 7.0% is simply impossible.

Producing a 2.0% wedge looks like it should be easy. After all it is a very small number. It is, however, extremely difficult to pull off. It is suggested as a goal for the same reasons that were discussed back in Step Two on setting a profit goal—it makes you stretch, but is something you can actually do with focused effort.

The last column of numbers is designed to give you chest pains. Slip a nitroglycerin pill under your tongue and take a look. In this column the figures represent a sales decline of 5.0%. If payroll can be reduced by 7.0%, that will also produce the desired 2.0% wedge. It is just off-the-wall difficult to do in a small business. If it could be done, though, there is actually a modest increase in profit in a down market.

Any time that payroll can be controlled in conjunction with sales (that is, generate a sales to payroll wedge), then profits can be enhanced systematically. This is true if sales go up a little, sales go up a lot or sales even go down. You're overdue for a homily: Sales are vanity, profits are sanity. It is not the sales increase, it is the profit increase that is important.

In the real world, sales growth almost always helps. It is a lot easier to put together the 2.0% wedge when sales are on the way up than it is when sales are on the way down. There is a need for some sales growth. Regardless of the growth rate, get comfortable with the "to do" of a 2.0% sales to payroll wedge.

Ignore This Sage Advice At Your Own Peril

In the heat of the battle, it is very easy to forget the 2.0% wedge. There is also somebody that will help you forget. That person is Fred.

You know Fred. He's been employed by you for twenty years. He stopped working eighteen years ago, but he still is employed. He's a nice guy. He has a family. He needs a raise. Actually, he needs a gold watch and a handshake, but it's time for Fred to get a raise anyway.

Exhibit 9 looks at the impact of providing that raise he so richly deserves. The first two columns of numbers are identical to the first two columns in Exhibit 8. They are the firm's current results and what would happen with 5.0% sales growth and a 2.0% sales to payroll wedge. This column has been labeled Scenario One.

The last column flips the sales to payroll wedge. That is, sales still go up by 5.0%. However, payroll increases by 7.0%. It actually goes up 2.0% faster than sales. The net result is that on the same exact sales increase profit goes down rather than up.

The two scenarios in Exhibit 9 encapsulate American business. Some years Scenario One happens, other years Scenario Two happens. Over time sales and payroll tend to move at the same rate. There is no payroll wedge. Nothing really changes in terms of profit. Your job is to make change happen until you reach the Maximum Profit Level.

Exhibit 9
Mountain View, Inc.
The Impact of a 5% Sales Increase
Under Two Payroll Scenarios

	Current Results	Scenario One Sales Up 5% Payroll Up 3%	Scenario Two Sales Up 5% Payroll Up 7%
Dollar Performance			
Net Sales	$5,000,000	$5,250,000	$5,250,000
Cost of Goods Sold	3,750,000	3,937,500	3,937,500
Gross Margin	1,250,000	1,312,500	1,312,500
Expenses			
Payroll and Fringe Benefits	750,000	772,500	802,500
All Other Expenses	400,000	420,000	420,000
Total Expenses	1,150,000	1,192,500	1,222,500
Profit Before Taxes	$100,000	$120,000	$90,000
Percent of Sales Performance			
Net Sales	100.0	100.0	100.0
Cost of Goods Sold	75.0	75.0	75.0
Gross Margin	25.0	25.0	25.0
Expenses			
Payroll and Fringe Benefits	15.0	14.7	15.3
All Other Expenses	8.0	8.0	8.0
Total Expenses	23.0	22.7	23.3
Profit Before Taxes	2.0	2.3	1.7

Two Real-World Complications

To complete the sales and payroll goal discussion it is necessary to look at two additional issues. They involve 1) your salary and 2) all of the "other expenses" that have been ignored up to this point.

1) Your Salary. You need to remember that your salary line item on your operational income statement is there only to remind you how much somebody else would have to be paid to do your job. It should be based upon labor market conditions. What you are actually paid is over there on the other set of books—the one your account keeps for you. He is still bitter about this whole process incidentally. Ignore him.

In normal times, the labor-market salary that somebody else would be paid will increase. Whenever payroll goes up you need to make sure that the portion of the increase that is management salary is accounted for.

2) Other Expenses. In both Exhibit 8 and Exhibit 9 the other expenses were given benign neglect. That means they went up and down at the same rate as sales volume. When there was a 5.0% sales increase, then the other expenses went up by 5.0%, etc. Candidly, that is a lousy assumption. It made the exhibits much easier to understand, though, which is why it was done. Since payroll is the big expense item, the primary focus needs to be on the payroll wedge.

In actual practice, of course, you need to control the other expenses as well. Luckily, you can more or less put these on auto-pilot and have them stay controlled. Most of the other expenses tend to have a large fixed component. As long as sales are increasing, then sales will automatically go up a little faster than the other expenses. You can't ignore them, but if you stay on top of them every once in a while, these expenses will stay under control.

When sales decline, all bets are off with regard to other expenses. Since they tend to have a large fixed component they are difficult to reduce when sales deteriorate. They need a very strong review in a down market.

The good news out of all this is that Exhibit 8 actually understates how much you will improve profit by a smidgen or so. Not enough to worry about. You continue to have one marching order and one only: Sales must go up 2.0% faster than payroll. Put the term 2.0% sales wedge in your vocabulary.

Growing Too Fast

Admit it. You would really like to grow your sales by 25.0%. This Step hasn't had any bad news for a while, so here is some. Growing too fast will kill your business.

If you grow fast, you will have to add new employees at a rapid rate. They have to be found, screened to avoid the hard-work challenged, trained to do their job, and motivated. It is a lot more work for you. You may also have to expand the facility. Of greatest consequence, you will also have to have a heart-to-heart with your banker. Since your banker has no heart, this is really difficult.

If you have accounts receivable or inventory or a rental fleet or equipment you use in the business or any other major asset investment, you have a built-in problem with sales growth. When you increase your sales you inevitably need more of these assets.

To see how excessive growth results in dull afternoons in your banker's office, gander back at the 10.0% growth column in Exhibit 8. As a reminder, the net result was that profit improved to $125,000. That was nice performance.

In the movie the phrase was, "If you build it they will come." In the business world the phrase is "If you earn it, they will tax it." Assume a 30.0% growth rate (federal, state and local). If you owned Mountain View, then that leaves you with $87,500 ($125,000 times 70.0%).

You don't get to take it out and buy a boat. You have to invest in the stuff you need to run your business. In the case of Mountain View that means accounts receivable and inventory. These two asset categories totaled $700,000. If they have to increase by 10.0% to support a 10.0% sales increase, then you have to invest another $70,000 in the business.

You're still okay, but a hunk of that additional cash from more profit got eaten up in more accounts receivable and inventory. It got eaten pretty fast by the way. The same thing happens in your business.

Now there will be some offsets. If the firm has more inventory, it will have more financing from suppliers. Despite this there is a central truth that is not well understood: The faster you grow, the more you eat up all of your after-tax profits in additional investment.

Time to determine the Goldilocks growth rate—not too fast, not too slow, but just right. That "ideal" growth rate for your business is equal to the rate of inflation plus somewhere between 3.0 and 5.0 percentage points. Isn't that arbitrary? Yes. It's also extremely realistic.

With an inflation rate of, say 2.0%, an ideal growth rate is between 5.0% and 7.0%. Such growth rates are fast enough to make producing a 2.0% payroll wedge a little easier, but not so fast that they will eat up all of your cash. You might even be able to buy a boat.

So what would Mountain View look like if it did this? That answer can be found in **Exhibit 10**. In that exhibit sales increase by 7.0% while payroll only increases by 5.0%. The ever-popular 2.0% sales to payroll wedge. Since the owner of Mountain View has not yet read Step Five of this book, both Cost of Goods Sold and Gross Margin increase at the same 5.0% rate as sales.

Most of the other expenses increase right along with inflation, but some go up faster. Some will not go up at all, though. The growth rate is assumed to be 4.0% for those factors—cruise control if you will.

The net result is that dollar profit increases by $34,000 and the PBT% increases to 2.5%. The firm has kick-started its effort to reach the Maximum Profit Level over time.

Exhibit 10
Mountain View, Inc.
The Financial Impact of
Systematic Sales and Expense Improvements

Dollar Performance	Current Results	With Improvements
Net Sales	$5,000,000	$5,350,000
Cost of Goods Sold	3,750,000	4,012,500
Gross Margin	1,250,000	1,337,500
Expenses		
Payroll and Fringe Benefits	750,000	787,500
All Other Expenses	400,000	416,000
Total Expenses	1,150,000	1,203,500
Profit Before Taxes	$100,000	$134,000
Percent of Sales Performance		
Net Sales	100.0	100.0
Cost of Goods Sold	75.0	75.0
Gross Margin	25.0	25.0
Expenses		
Payroll and Fringe Benefits	15.0	14.7
All Other Expenses	8.0	7.8
Total Expenses	23.0	22.5
Profit Before Taxes	2.0	2.5

The Improvements That Were Made:

- Sales increased by 7.0%, as did Cost of Goods Sold and Gross Margin.
- Payroll Expenses increased by 5.0%.
- Other Expenses increased by 4.0%.

How Do I Do That?

Nice question. If this were a seminar, the answer would be, "Well, I see we are out of time." It's not a seminar, so an answer is required. Darn the luck anyway.

There are a bunch of ingredients that go in to the payroll wedge cake. You need to think about them as creatively as possible. Five are most important:

- **Raise Your Prices**—This will be covered in Step Five. Don't say it is impossible until you get there. As a hypothetical example, if you raised your prices by 1.0%, there would be no increase in your payroll. You would be half way to the 2.0% sales to payroll wedge.

- **Stop Paying People for Breathing**—Salary increases can't be automatic and they can't be based upon some "Cost of Living" adjustment. Evaluate performance on an on-going basis.

- **Develop an Actual Plan**—Like with numbers and everything. Planning, if done properly (as will be shown in Step Seven) will actually force you to move towards the sales to payroll wedge that has been discussed here.

- **Stop Doing Things Nobody Values**—Most companies provide a lot of services. Your customers think some of them are wonderful and some are worthless. Find out which services are in the second category and stop providing them.

- **Sell More to Existing Customers**—Some folks don't want to buy from you. They are wrong, of course, so you advertise a lot to them and offer them price deals. It takes a lot of money to convince them you are wonderful. At the same time, other folks already think you are wonderful. Sell more to them. It costs very little.

Moving Forward

This list will get you close to the 2.0% sales to payroll wedge. Other things can be added as you find them. For right now, though, the first thing on the list was pricing. Time to deal head on with that gorilla in the corner of the room.

Get Control of Your Gross Margin

This step will introduce a concept so innovative, so creative that it will literally knock you off your feet. Here it is: Buy low, sell high. You can get back up now.

Okay, so everybody in the world has heard that one before. The truth of the matter is that almost nobody is actually doing it. Until the lesson is not only understood, but implemented, it is still something new and exciting.

Unless you can get control of your gross margin, your company will never be as successful as it needs to be. It will never reach its Maximum Profit Level. Never is an awfully long time.

There are a lot of elements that go into determining your gross margin. By far the most important of these is pricing—the "sell high" half of the phrase. Until the fear is taken out of pricing decisions, gross margin improvements can't be made. Without gross margin improvements, there will not be enough profit. It is a relationship that must be thoroughly understood.

Making It Up With Volume

There are individuals reading this book—you know who you are— who believe that if you can drive enough sales dollars, a low-price strategy can be made to work. In some instances that is true. In the overwhelming majority of cases, it simply can't be done.

Exhibit 11 examines the impact of discounting under two very different scenarios. The first one assumes that there is no increase in sales revenue as a result of the price reduction. The second one assumes that revenue increases sharply. Don't worry about which assumption is best just yet.

Since the exhibit focuses on some significant changes in sales, the proper expense structure to utilize is fixed versus variable. This is because, as noted earlier, when sales increase the variable expenses increase almost automatically. That increase in expenses cannot be overlooked.

The first column of numbers presents current results for Mountain View which you probably have memorized by this point. The last two columns examine the impact of a 5.0% price cut under the two assumptions just mentioned.

Exhibit 11 presents results at the total firm level. The conclusions that are true for the total firm would also be true for individual transactions, such as reducing prices for a select group of customers. The analysis simply is a lot easier to follow at the total firm level.

Exhibit 11
Mountain View, Inc.
The Impact of a 5.0% Price Cut
Under Two Different Revenue Assumptions

Dollar Performance	Current Results	No Revenue Increase	Revenue Increase
Net Sales	$5,000,000	$4,750,000	$6,229,508
Cost of Goods Sold	3,750,000	3,750,000	4,918,033
Gross Margin	1,250,000	1,000,000	1,311,475
Expenses			
Variable Expenses	250,000	237,500	311,475
Fixed Expenses	900,000	900,000	900,000
Total Expenses	1,150,000	1,137,500	1,211,475
Profit Before Taxes	$100,000	-$137,500	$100,000
Percent of Sales Performance			
Net Sales	100.0	100.0	100.0
Cost of Goods Sold	75.0	78.9	78.9
Gross Margin	25.0	21.1	21.1
Variable Expenses			
Fixed Expenses	5.0	5.0	5.0
Total Expenses	18.0	18.9	14.4
	23.0	23.9	19.4
Profit Before Taxes	2.0	-2.9	1.6

What You Need to Know About the Numbers:

- With the 5.0% price cut, the new gross margin becomes   21.1%
- The dollar sales increase required to maintain dollar profit is   24.6%

1) No increase in Sales Revenue. The first two items under the first scenario (no sales increase) are almost all that need to be known. Net sales declines by 5.0% because of the price cut, while cost of goods sold remains exactly the same as it was. As a result, all of the decrease in sales volume becomes a decrease in gross margin. It is a dollar for dollar relationship.

There is some minor relief on the variable expense side as these expenses decline right along with sales. The fixed expenses, which are the larger chunk, do not decline, though. The collision of rapidly declining gross margin and slowly declining expenses creates a profitability disaster.

Profit falls from the current $100,000 level to a loss of $137,500. The company produces a discouraging negative 2.9% PBT. In slightly different terms, profit is reduced by 237.5%. Hard to put a pretty face on it.

2) Strong Sales Increase. The second scenario examines how much sales would have to increase in order to exactly make up for the price cut. That is, how high would dollar sales have to go to keep profit at the original $100,000 level when prices are cut by 5.0%?

The mathematics in this column get a little cumbersome. The conclusion is extremely straightforward, though. The firm has to drive a lot more sales volume to offset a 5.0% price increase.

The key to this analysis in the last column is the gross margin percentage that is produced when prices are cut by 5.0%. This is best understood by retreating back to the first scenario (the second column of numbers). Sales fell to $4,750,000 while gross margin fell to $1,000,000. In this instance the new gross margin percentage for Mountain View after the price cut is 21.1%. ($1,000,000, $4,750,000 = 21.1%)

In the second scenario the gross margin percentage is also 21.1% as the same 5.0% price cut has taken place. To maintain profit at the original level of $100,000, sales have to increase to $6,229,508, an increase of 24.6%. It is a very large, very steep hill to climb. Possibly a slippery hill as well.

There is one additional item that should be noted with regard to the price-cutting scenario . As the sales increased by 24.6%, fixed expenses did not increase at all. This goes back to a theme first presented in Step One. If sales can be increased by 24.6% without increasing fixed expenses, then the fixed expenses are 24.6% too fat. It's either time to trim or admit that 24.6% is impossible.

Truth in analysis requires noting that the exhibit says nothing about the demand curve. With a 5.0% price cut, sales may or may not increase by 24.6%. The highly painful experiences of a lot of firms suggest that such a major sales increase is very unlikely.

Cutting Price Even More

Exhibit 12 takes the analysis in Exhibit 11 to its logical conclusion. It examines the sales increase that would be required to maintain profit at all price cut levels ranging from 0.0% up to 10.0%. At every point on the solid line in Exhibit 12 profit remains where it was originally, which was $100,000.

The mathematically astute reader will discern that this ain't no straight line. As price cuts get larger, things begin to get even more desperate. At the 5.0% price cut level, dollar sales had to increase by 24.6%. When the price cut is doubled to 10.0% the sales increase required to maintain the current level of profit almost triples, ending up at 71.4%.

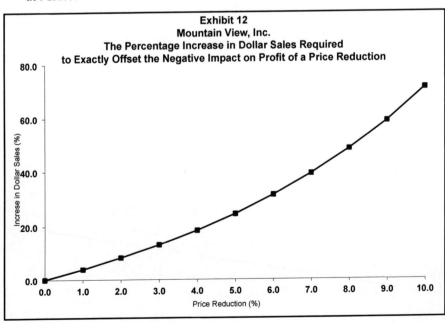

Exhibit 12
Mountain View, Inc.
The Percentage Increase in Dollar Sales Required
to Exactly Offset the Negative Impact on Profit of a Price Reduction

As they say down home, you can't get there from here. Firms with an exceptionally high gross margin to begin with might be able to make it up with volume as long as the price cuts are small. For most firms price cuts are fatal.

It may be absolutely essential for your firm to engage in serious price cutting because of competitive issues. In that case you must gut the fixed expenses. Not cut the fixed expenses, gut the fixed expenses. For most firms it is not a particularly appealing task.

Setting a Gross Margin Target

The process of setting a gross margin target is relatively simple. It also requires putting another performance goal on the board. Your gross margin percentage needs to increase by about 2.0% per year on any given level of sales. The gross margin percentage does not increase by two percentage points. This can be confusing so care is required.

Exhibit 13 (the world's shortest exhibit) takes this concept and translates it in to action. Mountain View has a gross margin percentage of 25.0% at present. If that figure is increased by 2.0%, then the gross margin target becomes 25.5% (25.0% x 1.02).

Exhibit 13
Mountain View, Inc.
Targeting the Gross Margin Percentage

1. Current Gross Margin %		25.0%
2. Improvement Factor		1.02
3. Target Gross Margin %	[1 x 2]	25.5%

"To Do" Number Two
Increase your gross margin percentage by 2.0% each year.

With regard to the underlying philosophy, it's the same old same old: this target makes you stretch, but is something you can actually do with focused effort. That idea is paramount to profit improvement.

There is one gigantic serendipitous benefit here. You only have to remember one number. It sounds kind of like Sesame Street—Today's profit program is brought to you by the number 2.0. You need a 2.0% wedge between sales growth and payroll growth and you need 2.0% more gross margin on those sales.

Buy Low, Sell High and Control In Between

Both "buy low" and "sell high" are important. As it turns out, gross margin is not a democracy. All factors are not created equal. In fact, selling higher is substantially more important than buying lower. Note carefully. Buy low is a very important concept. Sell high is a very, very, very important concept.

Exhibit 14 examines the bottom-line impact of the two approaches to improving gross margin. As noted from Exhibit 13, Mountain View's target for improving the gross margin percentage is to get to 25.5% next year. The exhibit presents two scenarios—make all of the improvement through buying better or make all of the improvement through pricing decisions.

Exhibit 14
Mountain View, Inc.
The Impact of Raising the Gross Margin Percentage
Through Better Buying or Better Pricing

Dollar Performance	Current Results	Buying Better	Pricing Better
Net Sales	$5,000,000	$5,000,000	$5,033,557
Cost of Goods Sold	3,750,000	3,725,000	3,750,000
Gross Margin	1,250,000	1,275,000	1,283,557
Expenses			
Variable Expenses	250,000	250,000	251,678
Fixed Expenses	900,000	900,000	900,000
Total Expenses	1,150,000	1,150,000	1,151,678
Profit Before Taxes	$100,000	$125,000	$131,879
Percent of Sales Performance			
Net Sales	100.0	100.0	100.0
Cost of Goods Sold	75.0	74.5	74.5
Gross Margin	25.0	25.5	25.5
Expenses			
Variable Expenses	5.0	5.0	5.0
Fixed Expenses	18.0	18.0	17.9
Total Expenses	23.0	23.0	22.9
Profit Before Taxes	2.0	2.5	2.6

Once again, since sales volume changes will be involved, the proper expense model is fixed versus variable. Also once again, Mountain View's current results are presented first. The second column looks at a buying-better-only strategy. The last column examines a selling-higher-only strategy.

The basic assumption in the buying-better scenario is that sales volume remains constant and that the improvement to a 25.5% gross margin comes entirely through improved buying activities—taking greater advantage of special deals, focusing on quantity discounts and the like. To achieve this goal, the firm must lower its cost of goods by $25,000. That entire amount will also be an increase in gross margin.

Since sales have not increased, there is no change in the expenses. This means the entire $25,000 goes to the bottom line. It is a significant increase in profitability.

The selling-higher scenario is similar in structure, but a little bit trickier to calculate. In the last column the cost of goods stays the same as it was originally. Prices are then increased so that the gross margin percentage reaches the 25.5% level. The important point here is that while the gross margin percentage is the same with either strategy, the gross margin dollars are higher under the selling-higher scenario because there are more sales dollars.

With higher sales there is a modest increase in expenses because the variable expenses go up right along with sales. When the smoke clears, the bottom-line profit is $131,879 under this scenario. Both strategies are good; pricing is simply a little better. Every firm is like that, including yours.

The case for the dominance of selling higher can be made in one more way. Buying lower is tough. Selling higher is easy, at least theoretically.

Buying at lower prices requires some serious negotiation if you are purchasing merchandise. If you are buying labor, such as technician time, buying lower is dependent upon labor market conditions and may be impossible.

Selling higher simply involves doing it. That, of course, is one massive hurdle for many people. The topic will be discussed in greater detail in a few pages. For now remember that suppliers don't have to be involved in raising prices. It is a unilateral action. It is also the most profitable action.

The Margin Squeeze

Small to medium-sized businesses often tend to get caught in a terrifying margin squeeze. The nature of the squeeze is that 1) the prices paid to suppliers are somewhat difficult to control (as was just pointed out) and 2) raising prices outbound seems to always result in complaints from customers.

The first problem is largely unavoidable. Suppliers do what suppliers do with regard to their prices. On the outbound side, though, firms are almost always overly sensitive to price competition. Such competition is serious, but can be overcome with some effort. For right now, though, the margin squeeze is on.

Exhibit 15 examines the nature of the margin squeeze and the massive advantages that arise when the squeeze is successfully avoided. After the obligatory current results in the first column of numbers, the next two review price increases both inbound from suppliers and outbound to customers. Please note that nothing is going on in these two columns except for price increases. Nothing really does mean nothing.

In both of the last two columns cost of goods has increased as suppliers have raised their prices by 5.0%. Specifically, cost of goods has increased from $3,750,000 originally to $3,937,500. As noted before, nothing is happening except price increases. This is not purchasing more, this is paying more for the same quantity of goods.

In the middle column the firm has raised prices by 3.0% out of concern for competition. To review, cost of goods are up by 5.0%, from $3,750,000 to $3,937,500. Sales only increase by 3.0%, from $5,000,000 to $5,150,000. Once again, it is essential to note that all of the changes are due to pricing.

In this scenario the bottom line is destroyed. Profit is almost cut in half. It is a situation that absolutely must be avoided. There is no scenario that allows the firm to absorb a significant price increase and hold the line on profit.

In the final column both cost of goods and sales increase by the same 5.0%. The firm has somehow managed to raise outbound prices in conjunction with supplier price increases. Now the opposite happens; profit explodes. Profit increases to $150,000 without doing any more work. The entire increase comes from matching outbound price increases to inbound price increases.

Exhibit 15
Mountain View, Inc.
The Impact of a 5.0% Increase in Cost of Goods Sold
With Two Different Outbound Price Increase Levels

Dollar Performance	Current	3% Price Increase	5% Price Increase
Net Sales	$5,000,000	$5,150,000	$5,250,000
Cost of Goods Sold	3,750,000	3,937,500	3,937,500
Gross Margin	1,250,000	1,212,500	1,312,500
Expenses			
Variable Expenses	250,000	257,500	262,500
Fixed Expenses	900,000	900,000	900,000
Total Expenses	1,150,000	1,157,500	1,162,500
Profit Before Taxes	$100,000	$55,000	$150,000
Percent of Sales Performance			
Net Sales	100.0	100.0	100.0
Cost of Goods Sold	75.0	76.5	75.0
Gross Margin	25.0	23.5	25.0
Expenses			
Variable Expenses	5.0	5.0	5.0
Fixed Expenses	18.0	17.5	17.1
Total Expenses	23.0	22.5	22.1
Profit Before Taxes	2.0	1.1	2.9

Everybody likes to grouse when suppliers raise prices. The reality is that such price increases are your friend if you can pass them along. They are probably the fastest way to drive more profit to the bottom line.

One final note. The price increase must be percent for percent, not dollar for dollar. If inbound prices go up by 5.0%, then outbound prices must also go up by 5.0%.

In Mountain View's case, assume a typical item that costs 75¢ and sells for $1.00. This is how the firm got to a gross margin of 25.0%. A 5.0% supplier price increase on the 75¢ would be an additional 3.75¢ of cost. The selling price shouldn't be raised by this amount. It should be raised by 5.0% or 5.0¢ to maintain the current 25.0% gross margin. However, it is 25.0% of a higher sales number, so profit is increased.

Hidden Margin Opportunities

Buying low and selling high are certainly the Big Two of gross margin improvement. However, the Little Three also represent important

opportunities. To a certain extent these opportunities are the prover-
bial low-hanging fruit waiting to be picked.

- **Advance Buying**—Many price increases are announced ahead
  of time. You should always buy an extra quantity of those items
  that are certain to sell. As a general rule, you can afford to buy
  one month's extra supply for each 1.0% increase in prices announced by your supplier. When you have the extra quantity,
  implement the new prices as soon as possible.
- **Pricing Errors**—Even in large companies pricing errors are a
  nightmare. The problem is usually that an incorrect cost is in
  the computer system. Maddeningly, the cost in the computer
  is always lower than the actual cost, never higher. This incorrect cost results in too low of a price. You should cycle-check
  your pricing. That is, every month you should review about
  one-fourth of your items to make sure pricing is correct.
- **Shrinkage**—This is an antiseptic term that accountants like
  to use. Does it mean that the items keep getting smaller? No,
  it means they have been taken home for personal use. Proper
  security systems are essential. Every story about internal theft
  and fraud begins with the statement "He seemed so trustwor-
  thy. We just couldn't believe he could do such a thing." Con-
  trols are cheaper than theft.

Pricing For Profit

Suppose you have to take a long airplane trip. Los Angeles to Hong
Kong comes to mind. For some reason you are not sleepy, so it is going
to seem longer than ever. You also notice that your e-book reader is
broken. It's sounding more like a bummer all the time.

As you are about to board the plane they announce the audio/
video system is broken. A panic attack is imminent. You need a book
desperately.

At the bookstore across from the gate you find a copy of *The
Shadow of the Wind* by Carlos Ruiz Zafón (which just happens to
be a truly great book and, as a bonus, is nice and long for your trip).
However, the blasted thing is $14.99 and you are a price shopper. It's
too much money.

Luckily, you notice right next to it, *La Sombra del Viento* which
just happens to be *The Shadow of the Wind* in Spanish. It is only $9.99.

Should the fact you don't speak Spanish deter you from buying it? Does twelve hours of talking to the boring insurance salesperson next to you on the plane sound like cruel and unusual punishment? You pay the $14.99. Gladly.

There is a great truth that you and every one of your employees needs to understand. To wit, it makes no difference what you sell; it is never the same product or service. Never is one of those absolutes, but it is a sound absolute in this case.

Companies that manufacture a branded product clearly have a different product. Companies that sell services also have a different product as there are clear qualitative differences associated with services. Even if the firm sells products that all of its competitors also sell, it still is not the same product. Service, support, credit terms, and incredible personal charm make it a different product.

Despite the fact that it isn't the same product most companies still under-price what they sell. They do so because they really don't believe deep down in their heart that their unique product, quality service, great atmosphere and absolute guarantee are really worth a premium.

The lament is often "our competitors won't let us raise prices." If your competitors set your prices, shouldn't they also tell you how much to pay your employees, where to locate your business and everything else? Besides that, most of your competitors—to us a technical term— are idiots. There is no reason your competitors should set your prices. You must be seen as competitive, of course. However...

It is never the same product.

A Pricing Experiment

The next time you have to price something try a little test. Say you are a contractor quoting the price of a new deck to a homeowner. Or, you're a specialty retailer putting a price on a new pair of skis. Maybe even a restaurant pricing a new gourmet breakfast item. Any of these or any more.

Take whatever price you were going to charge and add 1.0%. Yes, go hog wild and add a full 1.0%. If nobody complains, you have just put an extra 1.0% on the bottom line.

You will, alas, be hyper-sensitive and anticipate complaints. If even one person out of a hundred complains you will panic. After all, you are now gouging them for an extra 1.0%. No you are not; you are getting the fair value that you deserve for an absolutely beautiful deck, the hottest skis on the slopes or a scrumptious (ideally salmonella-free) breakfast.

Price sensitivity is always much stronger in the mind of the company doing the pricing than it is in the customer buying the product or service. If you don't think you provide a great value, close up shop. That job at the Department of Motor Vehicles probably is still open.

Putting Everything Together

Step Four looked at the impact of producing a 2.0% wedge between sales growth and payroll growth. The resulting profit was pretty good. **Exhibit 16** goes to the next logical step and adds 2.0% more margin dollars.

To quickly review, Exhibit 16 incorporates all of the assumptions from Step Four. those were sales up 7.0%, payroll up 5.0% and other expenses up 4.0%. The exhibit then adds the change in the gross margin from 25.0% to 25.5%. The exhibit uses the "buy things cheaper" scenario to drive a higher gross margin as it is a little easier to follow. Sales stay where they were (after the 7.0% increase from Step Four), but the cost of goods is lowered enough to produce the 25.5% gross margin.

The result is that profit skyrockets (a fair term, all things considered) to $160,750, resulting in a PBT of 3.0%. Two small, but not easy, changes have altered the entire profit structure of the business.

That was so much fun, why not twice, thrice,...uh four? The power is in the multiplication. The following chart shows what happens if the changes are repeated every year for four years:

Year	Dollar Profit	PBT%
Now	$100,000	2.0
One	$160,750	3.0
Two	$229,427	4.0
Three	$306,867	5.0
Four	$393,987	6.0

Exhibit 16
Mountain View, Inc.
The Financial Impact of
Sales, Expense and Gross Margin Improvements

Dollar Performance	Current Results	With Improvements
Net Sales	$5,000,000	$5,350,000
Cost of Goods Sold	3,750,000	3,985,750
Gross Margin	1,250,000	1,364,250
Expenses		
Payroll and Fringe Benefits	750,000	787,500
All Other Expenses	400,000	416,000
Total Expenses	1,150,000	1,203,500
Profit Before Taxes	$100,000	$160,750
Percent of Sales Performance		
Net Sales	100.0	100.0
Cost of Goods Sold	75.0	74.5
Gross Margin	25.0	25.5
Expenses		
Payroll and Fringe Benefits	15.0	14.7
All Other Expenses	8.0	7.8
Total Expenses	23.0	22.5
Profit Before Taxes	2.0	3.0

The Improvements That Were Made:

- Sales increased by 7.0%.
- Gross margin percentage increased by .5%.
- Payroll expenses increased by 5.0%.
- Other Expenses increased by 4.0%.

The dollar profit in four years is almost four times as great as it is now. The PBT% is three times the current level. All from making the annual 2.0% changes.

In the early 1950s there was a popular country and western song entitled Little Things Mean a Lot. It became number one not only on the country chart, but the pop chart as well. When it comes to finance, the idea of little things mean a lot is still number one on the profit chart. It should be number one in your heart. If not then your company's theme song becomes It Only Hurts for a Little While.

Maybe 2.0% can't be done every year. Any improvement that can be made in the sales to payroll wedge and the gross margin percentage will put additional profit in to your business. It is profit you deserve. Let somebody else work at the Department of Motor Vehicles.

Moving Forward

The major drivers of profitability are now set. There is still some work to be done on the investment side of the business, though. Time for one more little step in terms of understanding profitability and then one step in terms of putting everything together.

Target Your Investment Levels Properly

There have been too many homilies in this book. Time for a bromide. How about one you have never heard of: Cash is King!

The phrase "cash is king" has two distinct attributes. First, it is one of the most brilliant statements ever made in the history of financial planning. Second, it is one of the dumbest statements ever made in the history of financial planning.

Now, this is subtle, but those two attributes are in some degree of conflict. That conflict is at the heart of thinking about investment levels. The nature of the conflict needs to be understood.

"Cash is king" is an absolutely wonderful short-run philosophy when applied in small doses. It is an absolutely terrible long-term concept in large doses.

To truly appreciate that the phrase "cash is king" can be right sometimes and wrong at other times necessitates looking at the trade-off between investment and profit. That, in turn, requires getting knee deep in a financial concept that requires an ugly formula.

That concept is the break-even point. Discussing the break-even point may seem like a detour when talking about investment. However, understanding the break-even point is essential to getting complete control over investment levels. Bear with the discussion for a couple of pages.

The Break-Even Point

Everything in this book so far has focused on making things wonderful, which is a splendid thought. On occasion, though, things can go south. When they do, firms need to be fully aware of how far south they can go before they begin to feel real pain. That threshold can be measured by the break-even point (BEP).

The BEP is just as it sounds; it is that level of sales at which the firm produces absolutely no profit. It means that sales have fallen so much that expenses eat up all of the gross margin. On the other hand, the firm is not losing money either. Instead, profit is exactly equal to zero. To get as creative as financial types do—the firm is breaking even.

To calculate the BEP requires only three bits of information. Assuming your accountant is now working for you, that information is readily at hand. They include (1) the gross margin percentage, (2) the fixed expenses for the year in dollars and (3) the variable expense percentage.

The BEP formula is laid out in **Exhibit 17**. While it may not be straightforward to you as of yet, it is certainly definitive. The BEP for Mountain View—to the exact dollar—is $4,500,000. Not a penny more or less.

Stop Everything One More Time

The Excel template that came with this book will perform the calculation in Exhibit 17. Again, though, it would be real nice if you fully understood the steps required for calculating the BEP. Just letting the computer go through the calculations deprives you of some valuable insights into your business.

There is a fundamental message in Exhibit 17 that applies to virtually every company in business today. Namely, every firm is extremely volume sensitive. The level of sensitivity varies across firms, but every firm is highly sensitive to changes in sales.

It must be remembered that at Mountain View, sales were $5,000,000 originally. At that level, the firm generated a profit of $100,000. Things were not wonderful, but there was at least some profit.

According to Exhibit 17, if sales declined from $5,000,000 to $4,500,000, profit fell all the way to zero. In percentage terms, that is a drop of 10.0% ($500,000 decline ⹁ $5,000,000 original sales). Any way you slice it, the sales decline is not large. However, the puny 10.0% sales decline caused profits to fall by 100.0%.

The key to understanding Exhibit 17 is to remember that the firm must cover $900,000 in fixed expenses during the year. This remains true until it takes specific actions to reduce the fixed expenses. Until then, every dollar must be covered.

In covering those fixed expenses the firm doesn't have 100.0% usage of each sales dollar. Off the top, 75.0% of each sales dollar goes to suppliers, leaving a gross margin of 25.0%. Another 5.0% goes to pay variable expenses. What is left is called the contribution margin (accounting terminology, sorry). In the case of Mountain View the contribution margin is 20.0% (25.0% gross margin - 5.0% variable expenses).

The net result is that $900,000 in fixed expenses must be covered with sales dollars that only contribute 20.0% each towards covering those expenses. A total of $4.5 million of these dollars is required. The sales decline, as indicated before, is exactly 10.0%—a decline from $5.0 million to $4.5 million.

Exhibit 17
Mountain View, Inc.
Calculating the Break-Even Point

Gross Margin	=	25.0%
Fixed Expenses	=	$900,000
Variable Expenses	=	5.0%
Sales Required to Break Even	=	$ Fixed Expenses / Gross Margin % - Variable Expense %
	=	$900,000 / 25.0% - 5.0%
	=	$900,000 / 20.0%
	=	$4,500,000

Sales Sensitivity

This is what happens during economic downturns, incidentally. Sales don't fall by 80.0%; they fall by 10.0% or even 20.0%. Such a decline is enough to drive poorly managed firms into oblivion. "For rent" signs pop up in vacant buildings as firms fall below their BEP.

At this point you may well be asking a basic question: "What in the blazes just happened here?" Not to panic, **Exhibit 18** should provide a large degree of clarity with regard to sales declines and how firms hit the BEP so quickly.

Exhibit 18
Mountain View, Inc.
The Impact of Sales Declines on Profitability

Dollar Performance	Current Results	Break Even	Taking Action
Net Sales	$5,000,000	$4,500,000	$4,500,000
Cost of Goods	3,750,000	3,375,000	3,375,000
Gross Margin	1,250,000	1,125,000	1,125,000
Expenses			
Variable Expenses	250,000	225,000	225,000
Fixed Expenses	900,000	900,000	855,000
Total Expenses	1,150,000	1,125,000	1,080,000
Profit Before Taxes	$100,000	$0	$45,000
Percent of Sales Performance			
Net Sales	100.0	100.0	100.0
Cost of Goods	75.0	75.0	75.0
Gross Margin	25.0	25.0	25.0
Expenses			
Variable Expenses	5.0	5.0	5.0
Fixed Expenses	18.0	20.0	19.0
Total Expenses	23.0	25.0	24.0
Profit Before Taxes	2.0	0.0	1.0

The redundancy in many of the exhibits is probably reaching your pain threshold by now. Despite that, it must be mentioned once again that the first column of numbers represents Mountain View's current performance. The relevant expense concept for evaluating sales changes is fixed versus variable.

The second column of numbers looks at the break-even point assuming the firm takes no actions to reduce fixed expenses. Net sales, cost of goods and gross margin all decline by the same 10.0%. This means the firm is purchasing inventory at the same prices as before, selling them at the same prices and keeping the same relative amount. The gross margin percentage remains 25.0% of sales. The firm is simply doing all this 10.0% less than before.

Variable expenses decline automatically because they are 5.0% of a lower sales number. Fixed expenses have not fallen because nothing has been done to reduce them yet. The net result is that overall expenses decrease just slightly. On the bottom line, profit becomes zero.

The last column of numbers reflects the fact that most firms don't just sit there and take it. They try to change their expense structure. The challenge is that many fixed expenses are difficult to reduce. People can be eliminated, although with great sadness. However, the rent doesn't go down just because sales fall. A lot of other fixed expenses don't automatically decrease either.

In the last column the company has taken some actions. Namely, fixed expenses have been reduced by 5.0% at the same time sales have fallen by 10.0%. This provides some relief, but not real pleasure. Profit only falls by 55.0% rather than 100.0% and ends up at $45,000. Some profit is better than none, but it is still tough. Such is the nature of sales declines.

It is worth noting that the vast majority of business enterprises have a BEP that is within striking distance of 10.0% below their current sales. This is not enough breathing room. Ideally, there should be something closer to a 20.0% gap. Once your firm moves towards its Maximum Profit Level, the 20.0% gap will happen automatically.

The Break-Even Point and Investment Levels

It is very possible that the slight detour to discuss the break-even point has caused you to lose your train of thought. Very understandable. To refresh your memory, we were about to examine how reducing investment levels and converting them to cash (The King!) is either a great idea or a terrible one. The break-even formula will do yeoman's work in that effort.

First, a truism. The overwhelming majority of firms don't have as much cash as they would like. They may very well have as much cash as they really need, but they sure don't have as much as they would like.

The only exceptions to this rule are banks. They have lots of cash. They also don't intend to degrade themselves by letting you have any of their precious cash. You are on your own.

Since firms really and truly would like to have more cash, maybe even lots more cash, time to ask a question. Why do firms need to have it? "Because it's King" really isn't a very good answer.

Cash: Good and Bad Reasons to Have It

Like a lot of things in life, the reasons to have cash can be dichotomized (sorry for the big word). Yes or no, good or bad, right or wrong. The reasons to have cash also fall into this either/or view of life, in this case they are both good and bad.

(1) A Truly Bad Reason. Most business owners think they want more cash so that when sales fall by 15.0% and they are losing money, they will have enough cash to pay the bills. Heartfelt? Yes. Brilliant? No.

What those managers are saying is that when the firm is losing money, it can use this stash to pay bills and end up with even less cash than before. Followed to its logical conclusion, if the firm keeps losing money it will keep using up its cash reserve until eventually there is nothing left.

If the business can recover to its previous level of sales the "cash to pay bills in the short run" strategy may not be as bad as it sounds. However, the entire focus of this book is to help firms generate more profit. If it does so, then the idea of needing cash to pay bills can be avoided from the get go.

If profits were—to pull a random number out of the air—triple the current level, then the difference between current sales and the BEP would be 20.0% or even 30.0%. Then, if the firm sustains a massive 15.0% sales decline it is still profitable and generating even more cash.

Hoarding cash to cover losses is not a great idea. If the company is profitable all of the time—in good economies, moderate economies and bad economies—there is no need to hang on to cash as a cushion against losses. Thinking about profit from this negative perspective is highly dysfunctional.

(2) A Great Reason. Successful businesses grow. Sometimes they even ignore brilliant suggestions, such as only to grow by the rate of inflation plus about 5.0%. Check back with Step Four if that suggestion doesn't ring a bell.

When weak, inferior competitors go out of business, their sales tend to transfer to the smarter, more profitable surviving firms. Sometimes the opportunities for well-managed companies to grow are simply too enticing to pass up. These strong companies need more investment to support more sales. Alas, that additional investment requirement may outstrip the cash available to them.

Those great companies may then visit bankers who don't understand the industry the great company is in. The great company asks for money. Since the great company needs money, the banker's logic is that the firm really isn't all that great. Ergo, no loan.

The fundamental need for cash is to be able to finance growth opportunities when they arise without being at the mercy of dim-wit bankers. It isn't just a good reason, it is a great reason.

Let's try two for the price of one—yet another outstanding reason to need more cash. Across every industry in the economy, the companies that generate higher levels of profit tend to pay less in interest expense. That is worth repeating. The high-profit companies borrow less money and pay less in interest.

Cash Versus Profit

Finally time for the conclusion. Every firm needs to drain what are called cash traps and convert them to cash. However, those same firms need to make absolutely sure it really is a cash trap before they start draining it. What looks like a cash trap may well not be one.

For most companies the cash traps are inventory and accounts receivable. There are dead items in the assortment which generate no sales. There are customers who use you as an interest-free source of financing.

There may be other cash traps as well. For example, equipment that is under utilized in the business comes to mind. Firms need to drain every trap. For ease of discussion the focus will be on inventory and accounts receivable.

The key to draining cash traps is to limit the effort to the specific part of the investment that is doing nothing to help generate revenue. In most businesses that is a very small portion of both inventory and accounts receivable. With too much draining, profits can be severely impacted.

To understand how reductions in investment levels can flip from cash generation to profit destruction, it is necessary to understand how a lower investment helps profit and how lower sales volume kills profit. **Exhibit 19** addresses the issue of what less investment will do from a profit perspective. The exhibit addresses only inventory, but the analysis is the same for any other investment category.

In the exhibit, inventory is reduced by a whopping 25.0%. In dollar terms that amounts to a $100,000 reduction. This move provides $100,000 more in cash. A check back to Exhibit 2 indicates that Mountain View only had $50,000 in cash to begin with. From a cash perspective this huge increase is nirvana.

Exhibit 19
Mountain View, Inc.
The Impact of an Inventory Reduction
On Total Company Profit

	Calculation	Amount
1. Current Inventory		$400,000
2. 25% Reduction	[1 x 25%]	$100,000
3. Inventory Carrying Costs		12.0%
4. Profit Increase	[2 x 4]	$12,000

The exhibit indicates that there will be lower Inventory Carrying Costs (see Step Three). That is, less interest will be paid (hooray!) plus there will be reductions in damaged goods, shrinkage and the like.

Unless the inventory is highly perishable (bananas come to mind),the ICC is probably somewhere around 12.0%. That means that whenever $1.00 of dead inventory is converted to cash, not only does cash increase, but profit goes up as well. For each $1.00 converted to cash, profit increases by 12¢. The $100,000 inventory reduction for Mountain View results in a profit impact of $12,000.

This is the nature of the payoff. The increase in cash is staggering in magnitude—cash was tripled. However, the profit impact is relatively modest. Nobody should sneeze at $12,000, but nobody should turn cartwheels either.

The Sales Impact of an Inventory Reduction

The downside is that such a large reduction in inventory might possibly cause sales to fall. Remember that the cash trap is only the dead inventory, not inventory that is generating sales.

Without some detailed analysis there is no way to know for Mountain View, or your firm for that matter, how much inventory is dead. What can be done for every company, though, is to see what the trade-off is between investment reductions and profit reductions.

Exhibit 20 uses the break-even point to examine this issue. Yes, there really was a reason why the BEP material was presented earlier.

This exhibit incorporates a couple of additional items, but it really is the same break-even analysis. The other figures included are the current profit level for Mountain View and the amount of profit that was generated by lowering inventory.

The current profit is $100,000. That number has been added to the numerator in Exhibit 20. Don't panic, it's all legitimate. By adding profit in the numerator, the formula now measures how much sales would have to be generated to produce a profit of $100,000. That answer, of course, is $5.0 million. Mathematically, it is $1.0 million (fixed expenses plus profit) divided by the contribution margin of 20.0%.

Exhibit 20
Mountain View, Inc.
The Sales Level that Would Negate
A 25% Inventory Reduction

Current Profit	+	Fixed Costs	-	Additional Profit From an Inventory Reduction
Gross Margin Percentage		-		Variable Exp. Percentage
		=		
$100,000	+	$900,000	-	$12,000
25.0%		-		5.0%
		=		
		$988,000		
		20.0%		
		=		
		$4,940,000		

Finally, the increase in profit from the inventory reduction of 25.0% has been subtracted from the numerator. The goal is to see how much sales would have to fall below the $5.0 million level to wipe out the $12,000 of additional profit that was produced by reducing the inventory.

The answer is that sales would only have to fall to $4,940,000. That is not much of a decline. "Not much" is defined here as a sales decline of 1.2%. Uh oh.

The exhibit shows that the two changes are equal in terms of profit. A 25.0% reduction in inventory is exactly equal to a 1.2% decline in sales. The only open question at this point is whether a 25.0% reduction in inventory will cause sales to decline by more than 1.2%. The provisional answer is yes. A 25.0% cut in inventory probably goes beyond truly dead items.

Time for another bromide: You can't sell apples from an empty cart. If inventory is reduced too much, the short-run impact is that you will lose some sales. The long-term impact is that all of your customers will begin to go elsewhere if you are routinely out of stock. Sales then fall to zero. Hard to put together a high-profit plan with no sales.

Setting Asset Reduction Goals

The cash versus profit trade-off is one of the most difficult ones that firms ever face. Every firm must deal with the challenge, and guidelines are hard to come by. Two suggestions can be made, though.

(1) Inventory. The inventory has to be reviewed on an on-going basis. For non-seasonal items, a lack of sales in six months constitutes a dead item. That item must be discounted enough to get rid of it. Even if it is sold below its cost it will generate some cash. It is cash you probably need.

Items that are still selling, albeit slowly, are not really dead. They actually represent a profit opportunity. The price of slow-selling items can be raised with some degree of ease. If sales ever do completely stop, however, kiss the item goodbye.

(2) Accounts Receivable. This gets a little trickier. A customer that pays very slowly is still a customer. A customer that does not pay at all is an adversary in a legal proceeding.

For slow-paying customers, squeezing may not be beneficial. After all, the customer still buys from you and pays you eventually. You are always better off to have such a customer.

The key here is to slowly raise prices for this individual customer. A higher margin on the customer's business will more than offset the cost of carrying that customer beyond normal credit terms. The challenge is to make sure there will be a slow payment rather than no payment. You can't afford to sell on terms of "net never."

Moving Forward

You now know everything you need about profitability in order to triple your profit. Perhaps a dangerous thought, but still true.

You really should do one more thing, though. You should commit to developing a financial plan. The final step will make it easy to do. Don't abandon ship now.

Developing a Plan

This step will switch gears and look at the planning process. Before doing so it is useful to briefly review the implications for planning that can be drawn from the previous steps.

Two points have been emphasized. First, small changes in the operation of the firm can produce large changes in profit. Second, most firms need to think about the same general sorts of improvements in their operation. While every firm is unique and different, they all tend to need the same type of improvements.

Little Things Mean a Lot

The first major conclusion is that relatively small changes in the Key Profit Drivers (KPDs) can cause profits to increase dramatically. This represents a classical "what if" approach to profitability analysis.

Exhibit 21 presents all of the "what ifs" ranked according to their impact on the PBT%. For good old Mountain View the current profit level is $100,000 or a 2.0% PBT. The rows below indicate the resulting dollar profit and PBT% if a 10.0% improvement were made in each of the KPDs.

The largest impact comes from increasing the gross margin dollars (on a given level of sales) which takes profit to $225,000 or a 4.5% PBT. Other factors scale down from there. All of the improvements are only 10.0%. However, the improvement in dollar profit for the big three (sales, gross margin and expenses) ranges from 90.0% to 125.0%. Little things really do mean a lot.

If there is still some confusion about which factors are most important, please check the Appendix. All of the calculations behind Exhibit 21 are contained there.

Exhibit 21
Mountain View, Inc.
The Impact of 10% Improvements in the KPDs
On Dollar Profit and the PBT%

KPD	Profit Increase	Total Profit	PBT%
Gross Margin	$125,000	$225,000	4.5
Fixed Expenses	90,000	190,000	3.8
Net Sales	100,000	200,000	3.6
Inventory	4,800	104,800	2.1
Accounts Receivable	2,700	102,700	2.1

Goal Setting in Key Areas

The second key point emphasized in the discussion is that there are some nearly universal goals that can be set for the KPDs. That is, firms in very different businesses can all benefit by incorporating somewhat similar goals into their profit-improvement programs. Three are especially noteworthy:

- **Sales Growth**—Increase sales by inflation plus anywhere from 3.0 to 5.0 percentage points. This provides adequate growth to cover expense increases while simultaneously producing more profit.
- **Gross Margin** —Increase the gross margin dollars by 2.0 percentage points. At any given level of sales this will generate a large increase in profit.
- **Payroll**—Ensure that payroll and fringe benefits increase by 2.0 percentage points less than the increase in sales. This allows the firm to reward employees while still moving towards profit improvement.

As useful as these goals are, they don't provide a consistent basis for planning. The problem is that none of the goals is absolute. They are great starting points, but only starting points.

For example, a 2.0% gross margin goal is not always possible. In some years it may only be 1.5% while in other years it can be 2.5%. The other two goals have an equal level of variance year to year and company to company. The goals shouldn't be abandoned, but viewed as suggestions for getting started.

Planning via "what ifs" means the firm has to look at one set of potential changes and see what happens. It then has to look at a second set of potential changes to also see what happens, then a third, and so on. The problem is that "what ifs" can be combined in a gazillion different ways. It would take a lifetime to work through all of the different combinations. It is not realistic to develop a plan via the "what if" path.

It is still true that "little things mean a lot." It is also true that the magnitude of the changes required is in the range identified previously. It is just that the trial and error component of the process needs to be eliminated.

The planning process requires a procedure that makes the activity much more directional. That concept is what is commonly called "Profit First Planning." Excuse the acronym avalanche, but PFP.

Stop Everything One Last Time

There is a second Excel template that is part of this educational system. It lays out the steps in the planning process. Be sure to load that Excel template on to your hard drive.

This book is organized into steps rather than chapters. To avoid confusion the Excel template divides the planning process into goals rather than steps.

PFP is extremely controversial among non-financial managers. The executives in a few firms think it is wonderful. The folks in a lot of firms think it is absolutely insane. As it turns out, the firms where management thinks it is wonderful make a lot more profit than those that think it is crazy. There is a moral there somewhere.

Before starting the planning process it is useful to take a detour to address why most firms don't plan. The reasons provide some useful insights into why so many firms are willing to accept inadequate profit.

Reasons Not to Plan

Please take a seat in the Profitability Interrogation Room. Admit it; you hate the thought of planning. In fact, you would rather stand on the street corner handing out one hundred dollar bills to strangers than develop a plan.

Congratulations. If you don't plan you are essentially giving money away. You are leaving money on the table in your business.

Even knowing that, you still don't want to plan. Why? There are five fundamental reasons. Four of them can be overcome. The fifth can be minimized.

- **Process Confusion**—If you don't know how to plan, then it is impossible. The Excel template that was referenced in the copy box above will walk you through the planning process correctly. The text below will identify how the process works, but once you have the Excel template cranked up, everything works as close to automatic as possible.

- **Difficulty**—Even if there is an understanding of how to plan, there is still the common misperception that planning is difficult. It is something that they do at IBM with lots of spreadsheets and MBAs running around. Once again, the Excel template will make it easy to do.

- **Time Commitment**—For a lot of firms, planning takes forever. With the Excel template the planning process requires a very modest amount of time. This is because all of the calculations and analysis are being done automatically for you.

- **Lack of Value**—There is an understandable tendency to feel that there is no benefit from planning because things never work out according to the plan. In actuality, planning by itself helps you generate a lot more profit. This is true even if actual results are a long way from the original plan due to changes in economic conditions and the like. The reason planning has value is that it forces you to think about the financial side of the business systematically.

- **Dull**—For some strange reason, planning is often considered to be a dull process. On this concern, the only realistic plea is "guilty as charged." However, planning is not nearly as dull as that Poetry 101 class you took your freshman year so you could sit next to that cute Pi Phi. Planning is a close second, though. At the same time, if planning is quick, easy to do and drives a lot more profit, the dull can be overcome. Actually, if you make a lot more money, planning might be fun. Okay, it is dull forever.

Four out of five ain't bad. If planning can be made easy and quick and it really does increase your profit, then you need to get on board. The following few pages will discuss a planning methodology that must be followed precisely. Once you understand what is happening you can open the Excel template.

The Planning Process: Thinking Backwards

Most firms don't plan at all. The employees simply buy things and sell things while management hopes that if everybody works hard then things will end up in good shape. Such firms are victims of the economy, competitive reactions, changes in customer preference and almost everything else that can victimize them.

For the few companies that do plan, they inevitably do it wrong. By far the largest mistake they make is to start the planning process with sales. It is not simply a mistake, it is a fatal one.

Why not start with sales? After all, there is yet another homily: "Nothing happens until somebody sells something." The fact that some of the things that happen after somebody sells something creates losses rather than profit is never mentioned. Nice homily, though.

The real reason that planning almost always starts with sales is that the sales line is at the top of the income statement. Starting at the top and working down is the very essence of almost everything in life—"to do" lists, baseball batting orders, mindless PowerPoint® presentations and so on.

The logic of starting at the top is so ingrained it is almost impossible to challenge. The fact that in profit planning it is beyond dumb should at least be considered, though.

Starting at the top leads to what can be called "profit by subtraction." The firm plans sales first and then goes to the next item on the income statement, which is cost of goods. Once those two are planned, the firm then subtracts to get gross margin. After that, the firm plans expenses. Then expenses can be subtracted from gross margin to get profit.

This procedure is the very heart of the problem: In this sequence profit really isn't planned. Instead, profit ends up being whatever is left over after the firm stops subtracting. It is classic profit by subtraction. The entire process must be scrapped.

Profit First Planning

The only effective way to plan is to start the planning process with a profit goal. To use the term introduced above, Profit First Planning or PFP.

This concept was originally introduced way back in Step Two of this book, specifically in Exhibit 3. That logical chain started by trying to determine what was called the Maximum Profit Level. As a reminder, that was the maximum PBT% the firm could reasonably expect to achieve over time.

The logical chain ended by suggesting that for most firms the PBT% can be improved by .5% to 1.5% per year until the firm reached its Maximum Profit Level. That logic still applies here in Step Seven.

Despite the inherent wisdom of striving for the Maximum Profit Level over time, the idea of Profit First Planning is routinely rewarded with the complaint that "it can't be done." The complaint is that it is impossible to know how much profit the firm can generate until after sales, gross margin and expenses are known. In reality the complaint is more of a "we have never done it that way."

The counter argument is that profit by subtraction never gets the firm to where it wants to end up. That's a pretty strong counter argument unless profit is viewed by management as being no more important than sales or expenses.

The process of PFP eventually leads to implications for sales, gross margin and the like. Namely, the firm needs to generate enough sales to reach its profit goal. In that context, planning profit first may not be all that illogical after all.

In any case, the way to drive higher profit is to plan profit first. That alone should be enough to encourage firms to at least give it a try.

The Remaining Planning Sequence

After a profit goal has been set, the process becomes a little more mechanistic. Not exactly plug and chug, but certainly a "by the numbers" sort of exercise. There are four additional goals that must be set.

(1) **Sales Growth.** As a reminder, it was suggested that growth equal to the inflation rate plus 3.0% to 5.0% was ideal. However, there are always situations that are outside this range. Consequently, there is a need for a somewhat more encompassing goal.

There is only one word that needs to be remembered to get to that more encompassing goal for sales growth: Conservative. As long as the sales forecast is towards the low end of anticipated sales growth, the firm will be in good stead. Overly-ambitious sales plans are always killers.

(2) Gross Margin. Ideally, the gross margin percentage can be increased slightly each year. The same word of caution applied to sales growth is relevant here. If the expected improvement is conservative, the firm will be on track to developing a plan that can actually be met.

(3) Expenses. After profit sales and gross margin are planned, expenses become nothing more than a calculation. If gross margin dollars and profit dollars are both known, then expenses must be the difference between the two. The allocation of expenses between payroll and non-payroll items will still be required, but everything is a calculation with regard to total expenses.

(4) Investment Levels. Both inventory and accounts receivable tend to grow proportionately to sales over time. The only issue here is fine-tuning any variations in the growth rates for sales and investments.

Quarterly Review

Once a plan is complete, most managers put it in a desk drawer so it will be safe. Wouldn't want to lose that puppy. The plan is never looked at again. If it was a really good plan, then some genuine value was derived from simply engaging in the planning process. However, the "lock the plan away" school of thought does not close the loop on planning. There still needs to be a control mechanism to make sure the firm stays on plan. Some real benefit is lost without the control part of "plan and control."

There are a lot of reasons why companies don't plan. There is only one reason why they don't want to check actual results against the plan: "We ain't on plan!" It requires finding out why the firm is not on plan and doing something about it. As unpleasant as that may sound, it is how profit is generated.

The Excel template is structured for quarterly review. Every three months it should be determined if the firm is on or off plan. If it is off plan, the reasons why must be determined and action programs to get back on plan must be developed.

It is entirely possible that market conditions might have changed enough that the plan needs to be revised. With the Excel template that capability is always at hand.

Creating Action Programs

The primary value of developing a plan simply is the process of doing the planning. In determining how much profit the firm should produce, how much sales it can generate and the like, the firm is forced to think about where it is going.

This process must always be supported by action programs. For example, if sales are going to be increased, then it is necessary to identify the three to five things the firm is going to do to increase those sales. It is then necessary to ensure that those three to five things are actually being done. If this set of causal relationships is in place the firm is on course to reach its Maximum Profit Level.

There is no way the Excel template can put together an action program. That is the creative part of the planning process. The Excel template can pick up the grunt work and make all of the calculations properly. You have to drive the bus, though.

Moving Forward

You've covered a lot of ground. You have also put up with a lot of bad humor. However, if you have taken the materials to heart, you have the basis for generating the profit you deserve.

A strong motivation for setting up a business is the personal freedom and psychic income that comes with the entrepreneurial spirit. If you generate a lot of profit at the same time, that spirit is enhanced, not harmed.

Good luck in producing the Maximum Profit Level.

To Do List

(Actually a Must Do List)

So now that you have read the book, you think the profits are going to start piling up as high as you can reach and as far as the eye can see.

Not until you do something. You need to check off every item on this list. Slowly, if you like, but systematically.

Let me give you some bad news. Out of every 100 people who read this book, only about ten will actually complete this check list and change their lives. You will make the decision as to whether or not you are one of the ten.

1. Calculate your real profit using your best guess of local market salary and fringe benefit conditions. Now you know where you are starting from (See Step One in *Triple Your Profit!*).

2. Estimate your fixed and variable expenses (guess if you need to). This will help you understand the volume sensitivity of your firm (See Step One).

3. Set a goal for where you want your firm to be in five years in terms of profit (See Exhibit 3 in Step Two). Review this as a motivational tool every month.

4. Actually develop a plan using the Excel planning worksheet provided. Do this about six weeks before your next fiscal year begins. Update it about three weeks before the year begins (See Step Seven for details).

5. Review actual versus planned results three days after the end of every quarter. If you are off plan develop an action program to get back on plan (See Step Seven).

6. Review the profit sensitivities in your business to make sure you always keep them in mind. Do this every two weeks. Yes, every two weeks (See Step Three).

7. Read the free Profit Improvement Reports when they come out every quarter. If you don't get them go to: tripleyourprofitbook.com

Some Reminders Regarding Sales Volume

1. It is not necessary to increase sales dramatically. A sales increase of around the inflation rate plus three to five percent is sufficient.

2. Growing too fast is actually worse than growing too slow. It drains the firm's capital, beats up its employees, and strains relationships with suppliers and customers.

3. The most cost-effective way to increase sales is to sell more of existing products to existing customers. This opportunity should be completely mined before moving on to other strategies.

4. Raising your prices thoughtfully is by far the best way to increase sales volume. It requires no more effort and no more expense.

5. Since sales volume will not come automatically even if you follow all of the sage advice, carefully and objectively analyze the strengths and weaknesses of your competition. At some point you will probably have to steal sales volume from them. Hit them where they are weakest.

6. Don't be afraid to tell customers how wonderful you are. No need to brag all the time, but when you go the extra mile, point it out nicely.

Some Reminders Regarding Gross Margin

1. Gross margin is the single most important driver of profitability. It must be given first priority in all of your thinking.

2. There are numerous ways to increase gross margin, including opportunistic buying from suppliers, systems to control damage, theft and the like. They must all be used.

3. As important as everything else is, price is by far the most important factor in increasing the gross margin percentage.

4. Raising your prices in a thoughtful way also has a positive impact on your sales volume. This is two for the price of one.

5. On key items your prices must be one hundred percent competitive. If you are high priced on key items you are doing the same thing as renting a billboard on the Interstate Highway and announcing, "we are high priced on everything that we sell."

6. On slower-selling items there are numerous opportunities to raise prices. Do not be afraid to experiment with raising prices.

Some Reminders Regarding Expense Control

1. Expenses do not have to be reduced. In fact, expenses tend to go up continually over time. The key is to control them as they increase.

2. Payroll is the key expense category. There is no way to get control of expenses without making improvements in payroll.

3. The major objective is to drive a two percent wedge between the rate of sales growth and payroll expense growth. Again, this does not involve reducing anybody's wages.

4. One easy way to get control of payroll is to stop doing things that none of your customers view as having value.

5. Most employees are doing a great job. However, the vast majority of business owners are reluctant to terminate employees who are simply not contributing. It is necessary to stop paying people for breathing.

Appendix

Mountain View, Inc.
The Impact of Changes in the Key Profit Drivers
On Dollar Profit and the PBT%

The Impact of a Sales Increase
On Profit and the PBT%

	Calculation	Amount
1. Net Sales--Current		$5,000,000
2. 10% Increase in Sales	[1 x 10%]	$500,000
3. New Net Sales	[1 + 2]	$5,500,000
4. Gross Margin--Percent of Sales		25.0 %
5. Variable Expenses--Percent of Sales		5.0 %
6. Contribution Margin--Percent of Sales	[4 - 5]	20.0 %
7. Contribution Margin	[3 x 6]	$1,100,000
8. Fixed Expenses		$900,000
9. New Profit	[7 - 8]	$200,000
10. New PBT%	[9 ÷ 3]	3.6 %

The Impact of a Fixed Expense Reduction
On Profit and the PBT%

	Calculation	Amount
1. Fixed Expenses--Current		$900,000
2. 10% Reduction	[1 x 10%]	$90,000
3. Profit Before Taxes--Current		$100,000
4. New Profit	[2 + 3]	$190,000
5. Net Sales--Current		$5,000,000
6. New PBT%	[4 ÷ 5]	3.8 %

The Impact of a Gross Margin Increase
On Profit and the PBT%

	Calculation	Amount
1. Gross Margin--Current		$1,250,000
2. 10% Increase in Gross Margin	[1 x 10%]	$125,000
3. New Gross Margin	[1 + 2]	$1,375,000
4. Total Expenses--Current		$1,150,000
5. New Profit	[3 - 4]	$225,000
6. Net Sales--Current		$5,000,000
7. New PBT%	[5 ÷ 6]	4.5 %

The Impact of an Inventory Reduction
On Profit and the PBT%

	Calculation	Amount
1. Inventory--Current		$400,000
2. 10% Reduction in Inventory	[1 x 10%]	$40,000
3. Inventory Carrying Cost*		12.0 %
4. Profit Increase	[2 x 3]	$4,800
5. Profit Before Taxes--Current		$100,000
6. New Profit	[4 + 5]	$104,800
7. Net Sales--Current		$5,000,000
8. New PBT%	[6] 7]	2.1 %

The Impact of an Accounts Receivable Reduction
On Profit and the PBT%

	Calculation	Amount
1. Accounts Receivable--Current		$300,000
2. 10% Reduction in Accounts Receivable	[1 x 10%]	$30,000
3. Accounts Receivable Carrying Cost**		9.0 %
4. Profit Increase	[2 x 3]	$2,700
5. Profit Before Taxes--Current		$100,000
6. New Profit	[4 + 5]	$102,700
7. Net Sales--Current		$5,000,000
8. New PBT%	[6] 7]	2.1 %

---

* Inventory Carrying Cost

The Inventory Carrying Cost (ICC) is the cost of having inventory on hand for a full year. It is expressed as a percent of the inventory value and includes interest, obsolescence, some shrinkage, the cost of counting the inventory and the like.

As a quick approximation, the ICC is equal to the interest rate plus 5.0%. This means the ICC estimate used above is:

Interest Rate	7.0 %
Incremental Costs (Shrinkage, etc.)	5.0
ICC	12.0 %

** Accounts Receivable Carrying Cost

The Accounts Receivable Carrying Cost (ARCC) is the cost of having an investment in accounts receivable for a full year. It is expressed as a percent of the accounts receivable on hand and includes interest, bad debts and the cost of hounding customers.

As a quick approximation, the ARCC is equal to the interest rate plus 2.0%. This means the ARCC estimate used above is:

Interest Rate	7.0 %
Incremental Costs (Bad debts, etc.)	2.0
ARCC	9.0 %

Additional Resources

It defies logic that you would want additional material after having read this brilliant tome. However, two sources might prove valuable:

Budgeting à la Carte by John A Tracy. A more detailed examination of budgeting issues. Covers cash flow and departmental accounting in some depth. A well-written resource that is occasionally a little heavy on the accounting.

Accounting Coach. An on-line potpourri (no make that a cornucopia) of worksheets. Accounting heavy and possibly more than you ever wanted to know. However, if it is an accounting topic that small businesses should worry about, it is here. Available at: accountingcoach.com.

About the Author

Dr. Albert D. Bates is founder and Chairman of the Profit Planning Group, a research and executive education firm headquartered in Boulder, Colorado. The firm works exclusively in the area of financial planning for small businesses.

He has written extensively in both the professional and trade press, including the *Harvard Business Review*, the *California Management Review* and *Business Horizons*. In addition he has written three books other than this one. None of them are worth reading. They were warm-up exercises for the big one.

Dr. Bates received his undergraduate degree from the University of Texas at Arlington and his MBA and doctorate from Indiana University. While at Indiana he was one of the first recipients of the Ford Foundation Fellowship in Business Education. Standards were much lower then.

Prior to founding the Profit Planning Group, he was a member of the faculty of the University of Colorado where he was unable to gain either promotion or tenure. Before that, he was a vice-president of Management Horizons, Inc. a now-defunct consulting firm.

He is married and has three grown daughters. Their college bills are still not paid off, which is why he wrote this book. His wife and daughters all have black belts in Tae Kwon Do. All complaints about this book should be discussed with them.

CPSIA information can be obtained at www.ICGtesting.com
Printed in the USA
BVOW041652151211

278482BV00001B/35/P